A Better You and A Better CHRISTIAN

Samuel Williams

PARTRIDGE

To order additional copies of this book, contact
Toll Free +65 3165 7531 (Singapore)
Toll Free +60 3 3099 4412 (Malaysia)
orders.singapore@partridgepublishing.com

www.partridgepublishing.com/singapore

Contents

Don't be afraid to put your "S" back on your chest.......................1

New mercies today 9

Your profession versus your confession 12

Why we can't wait...30

Allow the spirit of god to interrupt your ignorance...............36

Few laborers? Maybe this is why..45

Bravo! More! Bravo!..50

An inspired declaration of war..55

Seasoning verses reasoning 60

Ready! Aim! Fire! 70

There is only one true doctrine..75

Encouraging yourself in the Lord...80

Foreign object damage 85

I've got a new pair of genes..92

Giving up to God...97

God, we thank you!.. 102

Complete accountability... 105

God, you are one ba-a-add dude!!.. 113

The truth about the active and the passive voices...................... 119

N-o-w lift up thine eyes 126

Twenty-five reasons to continue the fight................................ 135

Some times since doesn't make sense.. 152

Just do you 157

His word is my truth.. 163

I'm going into battle; I need a few good men............................ 166

About the Author

Author, Samuel Williams, is a native of Wadley, GA. He is the son of Mr. & Ms. Samuel and Ruby Williams, II. He attended the George Washington Carver Elementary School, Jefferson County High School (prior to integration) and the Wadley High School (post integration) where he excelled in both academics and athletics. Upon graduating high school, Samuel attended Paine College in Augusta, GA where he majored in English and minored in history. While at Paine he met and fell madly in love with his one and only wife. The couple has now been married for nearly four decades. They are the proud and loving parents of one wonderful son, Samuel IV and one astonishing daughter, Shundalynn. The couple also has two beautiful granddaughters, LeAndra and Jordyn Williams.

Samuel and Sharleen currently live in Yokosuka, Japan where he teaches Advanced Placement Language Arts and coaches girls' basketball. An ordained elder, Samuel is also a very popular speaker and Bible Study teacher there. A highly sought after minister, prayer warrior and public speaker, Samuel is also a gifted playwright and poet. He is also the author of *The Other Side of Jordan, He Always Causes Me to Triumph, A Handful of Love, Mercy and Justice, Thoughts, Reflections, Poems and Prayers,* and *When Men Don't Cry*. His books can be previewed and/or purchased at Trafford.com, barnesandnoble.com or amazon.com. Samuel is currently planning the release of two novels during 2014; both of which he hopes to see on the big screen some day. Having worked closely with families and youths for so many years, he has now adopted the vision and desire to write a series of quality, family shows for television.

To contact Samuel Williams email him at <u>manifestnow1@yahoo.com</u>.

A Word from the Author

This book is dedicated to anyone and everyone who wants to become a better person, a more fervent believer and a better Christian in as short a time as possible.

It is the simplest of books. It contains no long and convoluted theological premises or teachings. It is does not require a doctorate to read, digest and even self apply. Its contents are so simple and straight forward that some may even define them as insultingly so. However, none can say that its ideologies and expressions are far too erudite, philosophically, psychologically, abstractly and/or institutionally grounded that he or she cannot easily and readily clearly grasp the meaning and spirit behind every sentence found in this book.

As unpretentious as they are, the simplicity of these collected writings will, no doubt, bring much joy, power, peace, enlightenment and fellowship into the lives of those who will dare to take their deepest spiritual meanings and teachings to heart and apply them to the daily routines of their lives.

The steps to becoming a better you and a better Christian are so meticulously yet lucidly laid out in this book that even if an unbeliever were to stumble upon it, even he needs no longer error in his ways.

Introduction

This book was the easiest of books to write basically because I was neither trying nor intending to write a book when I wrote it. Actually, it was at the insistence of my peers that the information contained in this book was ever assembled into what you are now reading.

On several occasions, I would speak with individuals with little more as my intent than to share my thoughts on their subjects. Many times before I could finish my comments, people would ask, "Why don't you write down the things you say and put them into a book?" Since I was merely engaging in routine conversation, I personally had never considered doing that. However, after hearing the same advice again and again, especially after making numerous internet responses to questions, I thought maybe I'd better wise up and listen to the voices of reason. As a result, you now hold the product of their insistence in your hand.

I wasn't really sure what to call this book, and the truth is I'm still not. But because I simply lifted its contents from my several internet posts, I figured it would be most apropos to give it an internet-related name. Initially I did just that, but as this project progressed I could readily see the need for a more accurate summation of its contents, intent and purpose; thus the rationale for its present name.

I sincerely hope that this book does not disappoint you, but, rather, that it inspires and enlightens you. There is much greatness within each of us. With that assertion science, medicine, technology, Biblical scholars and the world at large and in general agrees. The conundrum is not why is there greatness within us, but why is it that so many of us fail to display the supernatural greatness that lies dormant within us, yet its fullest activation is but a simple prayer and exercise of faith away. I'm hopeful this book will help you reach the apex of your God-given power and will serve to provoke you into your righteous boldness to employ it against all of the wiles of the evil one.

Special Acknowledgement

There is nothing more precious to a parent than his or her God, mate and children. At least, that is the order of precedence all things take in my life. And with the first two firmly in place and secure, it is the third one that I know address.

My Wife

Often individuals who do not do what you do, do not really understand what it takes for you to do what you do. Needless to say then, because my wife is not a writer, sometimes it is hard for her to understand all that I require as a writer, coach, minister, teacher, speaker, father, only brother and son, grandfather, and yes—husband and partner. However, admittedly, she does an exceptional job of granting and/or providing me with all the freedom, support and understanding I can could possibly need or want. And that holds true for each project on which I've ever worked. After nearly 40 years of marriage, she has come to understand and accept my love for teaching and writing, and she, over that period, has become my number one fan and supporter. Clearly the Word of God is 100% accurate when it teaches us that "The man who finds a wife fines a good thing". I thank God for my "good time" and pray for a special blessing over her life.

My Son, Samuel IV

As I age, I become more and more acutely aware of just how important you are in this family. I, like you, am a lone son. The continuation of the family's gene pool rests totally with you. But not just the genes; the leadership, the patriarchal status, oversight, and wisdom are now being transferring onto your shoulders.

As such, you are so much more to so many more people than you currently realize. I challenge you to come into the wisdom of how significant your life is to any number of people whom you will never directly meet, greet or socialize with. Then, son, with certainty, humility, intention and purpose, walk that path as the one that has been pre-destined and prepared just for you.

Bless, praise and honor God while it is yet day in your life, for when it is night no man can honor Him. There is no greater feat you will ever accomplish than to find and rest in the love of God.

SPECIAL LADIES

I cannot help it. I am a deep and unrepentant lover of many women. Literally, I was brought up to be so, and would not, for anything in the world, change that facet of my being at this point in time. As a result, I would like to publicly give acknowledgment and thanks to just a few of these gorgeous and impactful beings. First and foremost, as I have already done and wish to do again, I thank my wife for her continued support and inspiration. She is my constant source of encouragement, enlightenment, motivation, love and partnership. She is the "good thing" that I have found. Next, and another repeat honoree, is our only daughter, Shundalynn. I have always referred to my daughter as "my shadow" because of our close father-daughter relationship since her infancy. I am so proud of her strength, insight and courage. She is a brave and bold young lady, who is not afraid of a challenge, but whose heart is larger than any achievement she will ever experience. Then, without fail, there's Mom. There are no words to say how much I love and appreciate her. The only word that comes close is "Mom." And if you've ever had a real and loving mom, you know what is all wrapped up in that single syllable word. My mother is followed closely by my four sisters, Bevelyn, JoAnne, Patricia and Sonya. These are my guardian angels who yet see me as their "little and only brother" though I am full grown with children and grandchildren of my own. (Sharleen says they still spoil me.) These ladies are followed very closely by my paternal and maternal aunts who have been so inspirational and nurturing in my development. No matter my dilemma, all of them were always just a phone call away. And finally, there are all of my nieces and my two darling granddaughters, LeeAndra and Jordan. I am so grateful to every one of them and I love and appreciate and acknowledge them all.

A Special Remembrance

Mere weeks ago, I endured the pain of child birth (literally) as I returned to the States to lay to rest my eldest sister and the stabilizing core of our family, Geraldine Williams. Gerry, as she was affectionately known, was quite a woman. Her constant demonstration of love for all of God's people was her unfeigned way of life. She never saw a frown that she didn't instantly seek to turn into a smile. She never saw hunger that she refused to feed or nakedness that she would not clothe. Gerry felt that everyone was "huggable" and that altruism should be the norm and not the exception by people of love and character.

A silent matriarch of sort, Gerry rose early every morning for decades to fervently "cover" each of her siblings, nieces and nephews in prayer. Each day she prayed for them—not collectively, but individually and by name. She visited the sick and shut-in as well as those who were jailed. She served the homeless and the less fortunate. She gave out of her own need and not just out of her abundance. And, most beautiful of all, though painfully stricken with breast cancer, Gerry refused to cry or utter a single complaint throughout the entire ordeal. Rather, though in and out of cognition as a result of heavy pain killing medication, Gerry's last words before her transition into eternity were, "God, I just want to worship You," and "Bless the Lord, Oh my soul and all that is within me give blessing to His holy name."

Gerry was the rock of the family and a rock of monumental impact and proportion in her church, the community, on her job, on missions and everywhere she ever went. To have witnessed the awesome transitioning of my sister's spirit from this realm and into the realm of glory is not only a spiritual mystery of epic proportion to me, but also my practical assurance that if I follow in her footsteps, just as she followed in Christ's, I too shall have eternal victory on the other side. Yet, daily it re-affirms within me, the knowledge and awesomeness of a just and faithful God, who cannot error and does not fail.

It is with the love of an only brother and that of a kindred spirit that I humbly, proudly and lovingly dedicate every word of this book to you, my big sister eternally.

OUR PETITION

Blessed Law Giver to the Universe, we humbly submit this petition this day and request that each utterance of our supplication falls peaceably and pleasantly upon Your attentive ear and kind heart and that the simple act of the submission of this request today will cause the inspired words of this book and these teachings to eradicate the shadows that many have come to see, believe and embrace and permit this truth to redesign their self images and to reignite their forgotten knowledge that they were, from the genesis of things, created in Your image and likeness. We ask that You reveal the power, the purpose and the wisdom of Your statues and that each reader will not merely intellectualize these teachings, but will internalize them by way of revelation and will activate them by way of personal application and that they will realize universal truth by way of individual experiences. We bow to You and receive Your teachings as divine laws of the natural, spiritual and universal realms. Guide the minds, wills, inner eyes and spirits of those who truly seek Your power and wisdom in order that they may indeed become better persons in only a few days. We give voice to this petition and release it unto the eternal and perfect Law Giver, Creator and Sustainer of all things, knowing that it is by Your power and grace that the lives of men are eternally changed. Amen.

READ THESE PAGES BEFORE READING THIS BOOK!!

No one who is seriously seeking positive and lasting change in their life will experience it against their true will or disproportionately to their own efforts. People change simply because they are seek and pursue change and because they are willing to do whatever is necessary to bring about the desired change about in their lives.

Many years ago, while lumbering about in my own personal discomfort, an old friend of mine, Evelyn Harris, called me at. I knew it was a divinely inspired called because it was during the middle of the summer and, for the most part, I usually heard from her during my birth month of January, once a year.

Our brief annual conversation took many turns from family to friends to church to the conversation which follows. From the outset, I wasn't really sure just why god had moved her to call me and to say certain things to me, but as time went by, it became clearer and clearer why I'd received the call:

"Hello. Who? Oh. Yes, ma'am, he is. All right. I'll get him for you. Just a minute please. Dad . . . telephone."

"Hello. Oh. Hi there. How are you, Evelyn? Long time no hear from."

"I know, Sam. I know. It's been a while hasn't it? You guys were on my mind and in my heart so I decided to get up and give y'all a buzz this morning. The kids sound great—happy. I pray they are."

"They are. It's just me who seems to be in a new and different fight every day."

"Who are you fighting—everyday?"

"The man. The man."

"Are you still doing what you know you were purposed and gifted to do?"

"I'm getting there."

"And that's your fight."

"What do you mean?"

"The fight is to keep you away from your destiny and purpose. In doing so, your adversary knows that you are so busy and engrossed with him that you can never keep your eye on your destiny. And if your eye is not on your destiny, then your path of pursuit probably is not leading you in that direction either. You're fighting a winless battle, Sam. You can never defeat your foe with the tools you're using because they were never designed for use in a fight against your present foe."

"What?"

"What you are wrestling against now is neither flesh nor blood but a power which cannot be measured or quantified by instruments, capsulated by technology or comprehended by natural thoughts. You are fighting a fight that has been tailor made and released against you for the purpose of destroying your hope, denying you the greatness that is within you and stealing your joy and peace and replacing it with frustration, anger and depression."

"Evelyn, what are you talking about?"

"You are in a battle which is designed to attack and kill your faith, vision, power and purpose. You battle so hard, so much and so frequently because you are predestined for extreme greatness, but as long as you do not realize this, you will settle for a daily fight which you cannot win and which serves only as a rouse for the enemy."

"You're losing me. I don't understand . . ."

"No I'm not. Not at all. And you do. I'm not losing you and you do understand, and I know both of these statements to be true and you do too. Don't play innocent, dumb or unaware with me, Samuel Williams. I know you boy! And I know you know well what I'm talking about too. I knew there was a greater reason for the prompting of this call than to merely exchange greetings with you and Sharleen. I knew it."

"You're right, Evelyn. I guess playing small and uninformed was suppose to be my justification and explanation as to why I wasn't doing what I know I should be doing."

"Are you tired, Sam?"

"What do you mean am I tired?"

"You heard me. Are you tired? Tired of fighting? Tired of learning but never coming into the real and true necessary knowledge? Tired of fighting from sun up to sun down? Tired of living from pay check to pay check? Tired of turning left and walking square into a wall, then turning right and walking square into a wall, then turning behind you and walking into a wall. Are you tired? Are you tired of seeing the less prepared prosper while you just continue to fight your never ending battle of fatigue against a nameless, faceless enemy. Are you tired of being stuck in the same place on the treadmill of mobility and success? Are you tired or are you just frustrated?"

"What's the difference?"

"If you're only frustrated, you will seek to eradicate the source of frustration, albeit, perhaps it might be only a temporary but immediate fix. Thus, it is destined to return."

"But tired?"

"When you really become tired of something, Sam, you don't seek to momentarily or temporarily or immediately dispose of it. You seek to destroy it, to annihilate it, to permanently do away with it existence."

"How does this apply to me, Evelyn?"

"Because until an individual makes an unwavering, unrelenting proclamation that he is tired of certain things being a part of his life, he'll never take the actions necessary to rid his life of these depowering influences. Courage, dedication, hard work, trusting, studying, believing, exercising discipline and many more steps are needed to overcome the habits, mindsets, negative images and traditions we have adopted as our destinies and realities."

"So what you're telling me is . . ."

"What I'm telling you is if you are going to remold, reshape, recondition, redefine, and ultimately rebirth yourself and re-resurrect your real destiny, the first step you are going to have to take is to ask yourself are you TIRED (desirous of permanent change) or simply FRUSTRATED (desirous of temporary and immediate relief from your current mental distractions and irritation.) Each will lead you to a distinct yet separate course of action and will yield distinct and separate benefits in your life."

"So what should I do?"

"First, honestly decide. Secondly, fervently pursue. The choice is yours. The results are your. The benefits are yours. It's all a matter of what you want for your own life and destiny. Think about it and call me back and let's discuss your decision. Blessings."

"Good to hear from you."

"My greetings to the family."

AM I HONESTLY TIRED
OR THOROUGHLY FRUSTRATED?

Changing is hard enough to do even when you've firmly decided that it's something that you really want to and need to do. So the one thing you do not want to have to deal with or have to hamper your change progress is indecisiveness. Before you can truly change, you must first come to a firm and fixed decision within yourself that change—real change—is what you truly desire, are pursuing and won't stop until you achieve.

"A CHANGE IS NOT A CHANGE UNTIL YOU CHANGE"

Many people fail to achieve change because what they really want is only temporary relief, immediate gratification, momentary reprisal or even a respite from their current circumstances. But none of these is a true and permanent life altering change. You see "A CHANGE IS NOT A CHANGE UNTIL YOU CHANGE." Settling is not changing. Seeking a more comfortable place in life is not necessarily a change, though it might require change in order to achieve. To change is to replace one thing with another, to give up something in order to gain or become something new, something different. You cannot remain as you are and be changed into what you wish to become at the same time. Change requires that we vacate our comfort zones, face our fears, give voice to expectations, raise our level of faith, eradicate the stronghold of traditions and forget those mistakes of yesterday that caused us to see ourselves as failures. Change mandates that we exercise the boldness and conviction to reach into our futures ourselves with the intent to take hold of our own dreams, desires and aspirations. Change causes us to re-evaluate our words and to re-focus our visions. It makes those of us who wish to become something new and different refuse to accept the standard of status quo and it forces us to take seriously the teaching of one great man who wrote:

> Out of the night that covers me
> Dark as a pit from pole to pole
> I thank whatever gods there may be
> For my unconquerable soul
> In the fell clutch of circumstance
> I have no winced nor cried aloud
> Under the bludgeoning of chance
> My head is bloodied but unbowed
> It matters not how strait the gate
> Or how charged with punishment the scroll
> I am the master of my faith
> I am the captain of my soul

Change requires, then, in a single word, courage. Moreover, though, it demands decisiveness on the part of the would-be-changed. When we speak of change, we speak of a permanent altering of what presently exists. Which, in essence, means once the change has occurred that which now is shall be no more. That is why we must first and foremost firmly affix our minds upon the massive and powerful question, "Am I tired or just frustrated?" Why? Because tired people want change. Frustrated people only want a momentary break.

When abused spouses are merely frustrated, they continue to return to their abusive partners. But when they become tired, they do whatever is necessary to change their status, connection to and relationship with their abuser. When alcoholics become frustrated, they momentarily stop drinking as much and as often (for as long as their addition will allow them to); but when they become really tired, they admit their problem and their helplessness to overcome it and seek professional assistance. When kids who are bullied become frustrated, they run, they report, they hide, they avoid. But when they become tired, they turn and fight. Sometimes they even become overly aggressive. Why? Because they are tired of the problem that has nagged, terrorized, and robbed them by denying them of the right to be all that they are capable of being. They are no longer willing to stand by helplessly and fearfully and continue to be drained of their strength, happiness and inalienable rights. They are no longer willing to tolerate the existence of such a force in their universe. And so they turn and fight with the intention and resolve to permanently change a negative situation into a positive one in their lives. But they do so only because and when they have grown tired.

"Genuine change of any kind demands courage."

Today, you must first settle within your mind and your heart which of these two characteristics better describes your current status today. Are you tired or are you frustrated? Because frustration will not allow you to latch onto the determination—long term, unrelenting determination—which is vitally essential for you if you are to bring about a situation-altering, permanent change in your life. Sure, frustration will yield you immediate gratification, but like a shrub whose undesired and unsightly branches have been pruned away, your problems are certain to return because as long as there are strong and healthy roots to provide nourishment, the branches (though pruned) will continue to sprout. Shortly after the temporary results of frustration have fully run their course, thereafter you will discover that despite a well-intentioned job of pruning, inevitably and unavoidably limbs that are nourished will re-sprout. On the other hand, if the shrub is excavated in its entirety there exists no possibility of its return. If the shrub which gives life to the limbs is removed at the root level, there will remain no part of it which is capable of re-supplying life sustaining nutrients to the branches. In other words, being tired will allow you to deal with the problem from a root-removal basis while being frustrated will only permit you to deal with the branches. Now if branch pruning is all that you are seeking, then by all means prune your branches. But if root removal is what you seek, then you must decide today that it is the root and the root only (a permanent and long term positive, life altering change) which you seek and will settle for.

This is a decision that no one else in the entire universe can make for you. It is a decision that you must make based upon your level of sincerity and personal commitment to your own goal. It is the single most critical decision you can make if you are going to re-make you because without the absolute commitment of a firm decision upon which you will have to stand, operate, speak and believe, you cannot move any further toward the goal of real change.

If you are "ify" about it, then you have not yet decided that real change is what you want. If you are not yet tired, then achieving real change could be a doubtful task for you. If you are frustrated, then real and lasting change is not what you are looking for right now. This is one decision you must make up in your mind, settle in your heart and pursue with all of your might. If you have never made a serious decision in your life, then I ask you personally, please take the time to consider the challenge of this simple question, "Am I Tired or Am I Frustrated?" Your answer will then let you know whether you are ready to take on the 30 days of this book.

There are 30 days of non-related life applications and spiritual belief materials in the remainder of this book. If you will read, believe, accept as truth and actively apply just one of these principles to your life a day, I promise you that by the end of your 30th day you will not believe the advancement you will have made or the growth you will have realized.

I pray that it blesses you, moves you to another level, and re-shapes you into that being you were created and purposed to be.

Blessings and enjoy.

Me

I know what you see when you look at me.
But do you know what it is you really see?

I know the fashions which impress you
and the words you like to hear,
But do you know the soul into which
your natural eyes can never peer?

Do you know my heart whose prayers you have never heard?
Do you know my indomitable spirit which cannot be deterred?

Do you know my hope which is the very engine of my soul?
Do you know my inspiration which refuses
to let me abandon my life's goals?

Do you know my past, my present, and my future yet to come?
Then you don't know me, because of
these things I am but the sum.

Remember This

God does not need, require or desire you as his co-pilot. If you are unable to soar with Him as your pilot, chances are very slim that you will ever soar at all.

Taking matters into our own hands is just a way of saying, "God, you're excused. I know You know how to best handle this, but I'm going to take care of this situation myself, in my own way. Oh, and by the way, please bless my rebellious attitude and effort on Your way out the door." FAITH—PATIENCE—OBEDIENCE.

Don't Be Afraid to Put Your "S" Back On Your Chest

REAL MEN WEAR "S"

I want to begin this book by sharing a word with the men. I hope those who have ears to hear will hear what the Spirit of God is saying through this vessel, which is: TODAY, GOD IS DEMANDING THAT WE—MEN OF FAITH—REGROUP AND REPLACE THE "S" UPON OUR CHESTS.

Yes, I know this sounds funny, but there exists a great need for the men of God to exercise the power, authority and wisdom that can only come through them when they are operating out of the power of their "S". Many years ago, men were told to remove the "S" from their chests and to recognize that they are not "Supermen". However, nothing can be further from God's truth than that teaching. Brothers, we were called BEFORE THE FOUNDATION OF THE WORLD" by God unto the performance and representation of His holy will and purpose in and for the earth. That is to say we were spiritually adopted into the family of God for the purpose of bringing Heaven to earth through our behavior, beliefs, and practices as a divine instrument of God in the flesh. In other words, we were CALLED or summons (aroused, awakened, given a name, purpose and identity, selected, ordained, fashioned, empowered and released) into the earth to perform unearthly duties, to exercise unnatural practices and to occupy divine offices and positions and to render supernatural services to those in need of a savior, a deliverer and a true and living God.

These things you can never do without the "S" of God being stamped upon your heart. Your "S" is not to indicate that you, in and of yourself are "super". Rather it simply acknowledges that you can do all things through him who has called you into the position of "Sanctification," "Salvation," "Saved," "Strength," "Security," "Sincerity," and "Sonship". Your "S" gives credence to your divine credentials and acknowledges the source of its existence and authorization in your life and Christian walk. It does not and should not ever be taken to represent "Self". Rather, it should always precede and exceed you and represent you as a product and ambassador of He and He alone who is "Savior" of all.

While your "S" certainly does imply and implicate you as a "Supernatural" being, rightfully so it should. For it is no longer you who lives, but Christ who lives and operates through you. Therefore, how could you not be a "Supernatural" being? Is not the God and Savior that rests, resides and resonates within you a supernatural being? For that you should not apologize, but glorify Him who truly is greater than a mere "Superman"! To HIM belongs all the honor, glory and praise. And to us belong the mantles of prayer, praise and service that we may at all times extol Him while we remain in our suits of flesh.

Men who boldly wear their "S" upon their chests are not ashamed to allow people to know that I am dead to the flesh. They are not ashamed to lift up holy hands and to pray in public as well as private places. They are bold to say no to the invites of sin. They can stand and rightfully occupy the office of priests of their homes and representatives of the kingdom. They are not too prideful worship Him who called, cleansed, converted and covered them. Early in the morning will the "S" men rise and seek the presence and protection of God over their homes, marriages, children, extended families, endeavors, ministries and lives' purposes. Daily will they crucify their flesh. Moment by moment will they acknowledge the greatness of their Savior. And day by day will they grow from grace to grace.

I have no idea from where the teaching of men of God removing their "S" from their chest came. But, I rebuke it in the name of Jesus, our Christ and Savior. For without the acknowledgement of my "S," surely I would slip and spend eternity in Sheol.

Men of God, go back into your spiritual phone booths and come out sporting your "S". Know that you have a special "strength," "significance" and "service" here in this realm, and that you cannot perform it by way of natural "strategy," but, rather only by the stirring up of the gift of the Holy Spirit that lives in you. Once you attempt to accomplish your divinely appointed mission without the aid of your "S," you have just embarked upon a mission of certain failure.

Go back. Pick up your "S" and don't sew it on, but PRAY it back onto the cloak of your spirit and never again remove the "S" of "Sanctification," "Salvation," "Saved," "Strength," "Security," "Sincerity," and "Sonship" from your chest! You have been seasoned by God through—by faith—your acceptance of His Holy word onto the rich and fertile soil of your heart to be and operate as the heavenly salt of the earth. But how can the salt season if it loses it savor?

Fathers. Husbands. Brothers. Sons. Men of God. Where's your "S"? It's high time you put it back on your chest and step out into the world wearing and operating in it.

Blessings.

FOR HE CHOSE (SAVED, SANCTIFIED AND SENT) US IN HIM BEFORE THE FOUNDATION OF THE WORLD. (EPHESIANS 1:4)

Pride is about you. Humility is about your reverence for and desire to be more like Christ.

Do Not Allow Pride to Dictate Your Treasures

(The Lord's Holy word plainly declares that He hates pride. It is an abomination to Him: "Every one that is proud in heart is an abomination to the LORD." (Proverbs 16:5) In other words, God strongly dislikes the spiritual condition of anyone who is proud in heart: "Pride, and arrogance, and the evil way, and the froward mouth, **do I hate**" (Pro 8:13). "An high look, and a proud heart, and the plowing of the wicked, is sin" (Pro 21:4). God is so much against pride that He says not only does He hate (the spirit of) pride, but He hates even the (prideful) look that pride produces in His creations. However, He does reassure us that "Though the LORD be high, yet hath He respect unto the lowly: but the proud he knoweth afar off" (Psa 138:6). "God resisteth the proud, but giveth grace unto the humble" (James 4:6).)

Brothers and sister, above all guard your heart with diligence. Why? Because out of the abundance of the heart the mouth speaks.

There is nothing the devil wishes more than to get into the heart of men. David knew this when he wrote, "Create in me a clean heart and re-new within me a right spirit." David understood that it is via our thoughts, our speech, our habits, our desires and even what we listen to that we grant the evil one access to our inner man. He seeks to insidiously enter undetected, unnoticed and unopposed. Check out the book of Genesis. How did he enter into Eve? Was it not by way of simple and innocent questions? Once she began to entertain the questions her resolve to follow the dictates of God was overcome and overpowered. There is nothing the devil wishes more than to get into the hearts of men. David knew this when he wrote, "Create in me a clean heart and re-new within me a right spirit." David understood that it is via our thoughts, our speech, our habits, our desires and even what we listen to that we grant the evil one access to our inner man. He seeks to insidiously enter undetected, unnoticed and unopposed. Once she began to entertain the devil's questions her resolve to follow the dictates of God was overcome, overpowered and re-directed. She began to justify, intellectualize and give logical reasoning to her conscious decision to vacate the directions of God for her (and mankind's) life. She toyed with the evil one, was insidiously deceived and gave all of hell the legal right to seize lordship over all that God had granted man dominion over and to release every form of torture, sickness, evil, violence and spiritual decadence imaginable over it and its inhabitants.

Once the devil brings evil and corrupt thoughts into your mind, if you do not bring them under the subjection of the word of God, that corrupt seed will then find a place of permanence in your heart (which is the spirit of man) and will manifest itself by way of your diminished relationship with God. Of course you will neither easily nor quickly notice the declined status of your spiritual walk. That would be dumb on the enemy's part. He must gradually lure you further and further away from your base (spiritual foundation) to a point that he hopes is the point of no return. How does he do this? The first seed he will most likely seek to plant is not a seed of rebelliousness, but, rather, the powerful seed of pride. And out of pride will come every other sin that can be brought forth.

Pride causes one to become un-teachable. Pride causes one to constantly compare rather than to support. Pride causes one to consider self and not kingdom. Pride is always about you and not about God. Pride causes one to say, "Look at what I have done, achieve, created or made to happen." Pride glories in self. Out of pride come lies, deceit, selfishness, intolerance, judgment, hatred, competition, rebellion, strife, jealousy, murder, lusciousness, greed, distrust, and on and on.

But we need to ensure that we check ourselves closely for the onset of pride because often pride is very much undetected and unopposed. Brothers, you cannot go around flaunting your "hard abs" because that is pride (of the flesh). And it is saying "Look at me and look at what I have done with my body." It does not glorify God in any way neither lends itself to the glorying of God. Check that pride and come in line with the word of God. Sisters, as beautiful as many of you are, please know that it is your inner light that God wishes you to show off and not your cleavage, behind, legs or latest makeup trend. You (we) are the Children of the Light; we are the off-springs of the Most High, and we must ensure that we do nothing to cause another to falter, fail or miss Christ.

If we cannot put ourselves, our houses, our physiques, our cars, our wardrobes and even our children, second to Christ, we, then, have a pride problem and God is not our God as He has given us His first commandment that we (which are His) are to have no other God before Him. And anything that we can't or won't arrest, rebuke, cast down, out or away in order that He may be made manifest, exalted, magnified and glorified in our lives, THAT THING is our God and unquestionably we hold it before Him.

Pride is such an evil and seductive spirit that it is often very difficult to determine when, where and how it has entered into our lives and our hearts. And, of course, the only way to keep it out is to repent, rebuke, bind (it) and release the redeeming and restorative power of God in our lives. Moreover, we must remember that pride comes but for one reason, and that is to separate us from giving God the glory, honor, praise and adulation He is due. Pride is Satan's number one weapon. Don't allow him to use it on you. Humble yourself under the hand of the Almighty and in HIS time, He will exalt you.

If you make this walk about God, and not about you, pride will not have the legal right to overtake you. Blessings.

Great is His faithfulness; His mercies begin anew each day.

(Lamentations 3:23)

Surely goodness and mercy shall follow me all the days of my life . . . .

(Psalm 23)

New Mercies Today

God, I'd decided that I won't serve You because I grew up going to church. I won't pray because of what I've been taught. I won't worship because of what I've heard. I won't surrender because of tradition. And I won't praise because it's popular. But I covenant with You at this moment to serve You, pray to You, worship You and surrender my all to You out of my relationship with You and because it is my heart's desire to do these things and more. I no longer want to appear—I want to BE. I have no desire to seem like; I want to BE. I don't want to sound as if; God, I want to BE. No distraction will ever draw me away from You. No temptation will sway me away from Your path. No enticement or offering will cause me to abandon Your straight and narrow. Heaven and heaven alone is my aim, my goal, my destination. Father, as I am unable to keep myself in the path of righteousness, I do humbly, willingly and totally surrender all that I am over to You, that you my keep my heart, guide my footsteps and Lord over my every decision. Shine your eternal light deep into the depths of my spirit man and illume all there that is hidden, dormant and disguised as righteous. And then, God, with Your divine precision, extricate it from my being that I might not look back upon it, give place to it or do battle with it ever again. Work a work in me, on me, and through me like never before. Give revelation where I previously had only sight. Give me Holy Ghost inspired words of power as You take away from me institutionally learned powerful words. Replace the sounds of havoc from hell with the melodious harmonies from heaven.

Empty me, God, that I might not leave this realm except that I am first emptied of every mission assigned unto me to perform here in the earth realm. Bless me to be emptied of every prayer, of every petition, of every sermon, of every encouraging word, of every written note, of every counseling opportunity, of every smile and of every encouragement and consolation I was designed, purposed, and uniquely prepared to deliver in this realm. I pray that You will move me to a new and higher level in You in every way possible. I am submitted to this supplication as I have believed every word, and, therefore, have I spoken and petitioned them unto You this day. Amen.

Don't Let What You <u>Do</u>

Determine

What You <u>Are</u>

Your Profession versus Your Confession

How ironic it is that in today's society we are often taught to hang with people who have big ideas, or to swim among the shocks, or to interact with those who have evidenced success in life. We are even told to shun those who are from a "lower" class or those who do not measure up to our standards. And while there might be practical applicability to some degree in some such claims, today I would like to remind my believing sisters and brothers that when it comes to Jesus our Christ, it was not His profession (natural job) but His confession (spoken acknowledgment) which made Him what He was to mankind.

In contemporary society we tend to believe that the bigger our salaries, the more assured we can be that we "have arrived" and are now rubbing elbows with the "big dogs". Conversely, Christ seemed to have a totally different standard by which He evaluated success. Seemingly His standard was based upon His obedience to the One who sent Him. He came into the earth by way of parents of no (prominent) name or status. He came to a town that was tiny and believed to be insignificant to the overall region, let alone than to the entire world. He did not arrive in a fancy setting or opulence. Rather, He showed up in a cattle stable, illuminated only by the moon and stars and was warmed only by the heat from a used blanket and the remains of uneaten hay.

His father was a carpenter. His mother was an unwed teen. He was a Palestinian Jew and a bastard child. He was not of royalty or of fame. He wasn't from a major metropolis nor does His history reveal any former schooling or matriculation. He never received a diploma or degree or was honored by any social or political group. History does not record Him having made any significant discovery or having written any prolific best-seller. He never experienced wealth and always gave all of Himself to the service of others as well as to the obedience of His Father's will for Him. The Bible, in the New Testament (the biography of Jesus' earthly existence) even goes so far as to describe Jesus as being unattractive in appearance.

Nonetheless there is not another single figure in the entire annals of humankind who is better known, more widely studied, more highly revered, or more remembered and taught than Jesus, the carpenter's son. Today, some 2000 years after His birth, the birth of His arrival among men is still the single most celebrated day on earth. His ministry is more powerful and prevalent than any scientific, mathematical, engineering, historical or social theory ever devised or promulgated by men. His principles are accepted and regarded as the only ones by which one can live a truly pious and divinely guided life. His doctrine is still accepted as the only doctrine to have been originated by and provided to mankind by God Himself (and not through a human vessel). His miracles and His story (His coming, His presence and His return) have been cataloged in a single book called The Bible and is by all sources, the most studied, the most scrutinized, the most widely printed and sold book in the history of the world and mankind. His birth is believed to be the return of God into the earth realm as a man (Emmanuel); His miracles all serve as proof of His deity; our acceptance of the truth of His gospel ensures us of our salvation (eternal life with God after life on earth is over); and His death, burial, resurrection and ascension all serve to validate the veracity of his teachings and our hope.

And He did it all without any earthly credentials. No man ordained or certified Him. No institution of higher learning graduated Him. No political or social group endorsed Him. Many in society scorned Him while many of others many mocked Him. The religious killed Him. The intellectuals scoffed Him. The leadership rejected Him. And yet with all of this going on in His life, He maintained His confession and His obedience to the Father. He never relied on His title, position or profession to empower or permit Him to do the will of Father. Christ knew it was not His profession but His commitment to His confession that made all of the difference in who He was, His effectiveness, His legacy, His obedience and our eternity.

The question then becomes have we become more concerned with pleasing man than with pleasing God? Have we begun to seek to associate with or be accepted by certain individuals or groups above being acceptable and pleasing to God? Are we still confessing ourselves as slaves unto the Gospel of Christ unto death? Are we still confessing ourselves to be children engrafted into the Holy family of God? Are we still confessing ourselves to be ambassadors for God? Are we still confessing ourselves to be vessels of honor and Children of the Most High? Are we still confessing God to be our heavenly father and the Lord of our lives? Are still confessing ourselves to be emulators of Christ Jesus and the righteousness of God? Are we still confessing ourselves to be the personification of the pure and never ending love of God? Are we still confessing ourselves to be powerful weapons against the kingdom of darkness? Are still confessing ourselves to be the salt of the earth? Are we still confessing that we are more than mere conquerors? Are we still confessing that our bodies are the temples in which God lives in the earth realm? Or have we begun to confess what we do as what or who we are (doctor, specialist, author, business owner, manager, supervisor, pilot, attorney, etc . . . .)?

Jesus, the son of an unknown, uneducated carpenter and an unwedded teenage mom, was wise beyond this trap of the adversary. He never became entangled by titles, positions, certificates or groups. He recognized that to do so would mean He could not be fully committed to that which He was purposed to do by the Father. Can we say that? Or has pride risen its ugly and dangerous head against our Godly relationships and divine duties?

It is not your natural profession to which God wishes you to be committed, it's your confession to Him and who and what He is in Your life that He wants you to be committed to. If you take care of your confession, He will give to you and safe guard your profession.

Seek ye first the kingdom of heaven, and all of these things will be added unto you. If you fail to keep your confession, you have made something else your God and have disobeyed this directive of this spiritual law.

There is no shortage of employment opportunities in the God's kingdom. The harvest is plenteous, the laborers are few. The first thing Jesus did was to give the disciples (new and divine) jobs. Mary, Martha, Paul, Luke. It doesn't matter. Even if they already had jobs or were unemployed. Jesus gave them new jobs, with a retirement package that is unmatched by any offered by earthly firms. Their benefits of power, wisdom, revelation, fellowship, communion, peace, joy and salvation, not to mention their names being recorded in the Lamb's Book of Life and a new home in (the New) Jerusalem where God Himself will live with them, clearly outweigh any benefits package ever assembled by any entity in the cooperate world.

These, too, are our benefits if we will endure unto the end and hold fast to our confession even if it costs us our profession.

Blessings.

A PAUSE FOR PRAYER

Father, bless us to speak only faith-filled words. Allow the words of our mouth to fill our hearts with confidents and our lives with joy. Do not permit us to speak words of defeat, disgust, doubt and destruction. There is supernatural power in our words. Our words are creative forces. They not only bring our blessings into the physical world from the spiritual realm, but they ultimately decide our eternal destinies. Please, Holy Spirit, teach us, Your people to speak with righteous boldness and holy confidence. Do not allow us to promulgate the language of defeat and doubt. Let every believer shout with certain victory that "I can do all things through Christ Jesus who strengthens me!" and that "The gates of hell shall not prevail against me!" Let every believer proclaim that "I am the righteousness of God through Christ Jesus and no good thing will the Father withhold from me." No matter the battle, let the rally call among believers be "I am more than a conqueror through Christ Jesus!" and "No weapon that is formed against me shall prosper!" Our words are our shapers of our destiny. They either move us closer to You or farther from You, but they never allow us to remain in the same place spiritually. Allow us to imitate You, Father, when You spoke into absolutely nothing and commanded the nothingness to produce all things when You said "Let there be . . . !" And all praises be to You, dear God, You saw just what

You said. Our words are much too essential and too powerful to be played with and treated little regard. They are the sound keys that open doors in the spirit realm and the rams' horns that give forth clarion calls into the halls of heaven. Teach us to watch our words and to use them wisely as they are a potent spiritual tool provided to us at the time of creation. With our words we covenant to give You thanks, praise, glory and honor and with our words we will set the captives free, cast out demons, heal the sick and strengthen the weak. Our word is one way we transfer the power that resides in us to others. Teach us, Father, how to properly and righteously use our tongues for their divinely created purposes.

Amen.

Let Forgiving Begin within the House of My Own Heart

Father,
Forgive me of my trespasses as I have forgiven
those who have trespassed against me.

Recognize that forgiving is always a choice. On the other hand,
its counterpart, unforgiving, is a major stronghold that the
enemy uses as a chief mean to steal, kill and destroy your ability
to walk in and spread God-likeness to others. Unforgiving is
a tool used against you to destroy your ability to love which is
one of your most powerful spiritual attributes and weapons.

FORGIVE US THIS DAY AS WE . . .

(Part 1)

Have you ever heard (or perhaps said yourself), "I'm just going to leave that person alone until they get it together because right now they're just getting on my nerves?" Have you? Well, what if God had "left you alone" until you "got yourself together"? What if He has said your lying, your sleeping from bed to bed, your hidden motives and intentions, your mean spirit, your jealous nature or your vindictive ways were ". . . getting on My nerves"? What if He had decided not to bless you or not to forgive you or not to commune with you until YOU'D gotten yourself together? What if God had forbidden His sun to shine on you or His moon to light your path or His mercy to precede your corrupt footsteps? What if God had snatched his words from the capacity of your vocal cords or His oxygen from your lungs because you "hadn't gotten it all together" yet? What if he'd recalled His mercy, been stingy and possessive with His love, selfish with His healing or discriminating with His compassion because you were still out of His will? What if?

Just the mere thought is a nightmare. Jesus taught us to ". . . forgive us of OUR transgressions (just) as we forgive those who trespass against us." In other words what the savior was really teaching us was to actually request of God to forgive our waywardness and wrong doings but ONLY AS we forgive those who commit trespasses against us. So what we're actually saying is, "God forgive me to the same extent, to the same degree, to the same level that I CHOOSE to forgive others." Therefore, if there is someone in your life who has wronged you and you keep saying I just can't forgive them right now, you have actually asked God NOT to forgive you of your trespasses right now as well? Why? Because that is what is meant by "as" in our model prayer. Literally it refers to reciprocation being made or returned in the same fashion or to the same degree or extent.

And so I ask, what shall separate you from the love of God? Will somebody else's harsh words about you cause you to walk contrary to God's law? Will somebody else's wrong deeds against you cause you to boldly and blatantly disregard the statues of God? No. We should all be saying NOTHING SHALL SEPARATE ME FROM THE LOVE OF GOD. In the fifth chapter of Matthew, as Christ is teaching, He concludes his message with these powerful words (vv43-45)*: Ye have heard that it hath been said, Thou shalt love thy neighbor and hate thine enemy. But I say unto you, Love your enemies, bless them that curse you, do good to them that hate you, and pray for them which despitefully use you, and persecute you; That ye may be the children of your Father which is in heaven*. Ironically Christ teaches us that to love those who hate us, to pray for them that curse and abuse us is not an option but a must in order for us to fulfill the earthly requirements for walking in our inheritance as sons and daughters of God in heaven.

So what or whom are you going to permit to cause you to come short of the honor or calling Him "Daddy" and He calling you "Son" or "Daughter"? Forgiving is a choice just as obedience is. But just remember, He forgives us JUST AS we forgive others. Funny isn't? How little old mankind actually determines just what our mighty God is going to do in our own lives. We forgive because we want forgiveness. We love because we seek His love. We show mercy because we want Him to be merciful to us. And you know what? He never turns us away just because we haven't yet gotten ourselves fully together. I don't know about you, but in my spirit, that's worth a big HALLELUJAH AND AMEN!!

JUDGE LESS—SERVE MORE!! BLESSINGS.

FORGIVE US THIS DAY AS WE . . .

(Part 2)

Unforgiving is a massively strong and controlling thing. It turns potentially good and productive people and relationships into mean spirited, venom spewing revengeful opportunists. The funny thing is that that which we hold, honor and esteem through the highly myopic lense of unforgiving is that which at this juncture in your life you've already defeated, overcome and emerged victorious over. The incident(s) never came into your life to destroy you, but to grow you up into the likeness of the Father, who forgives us no matter how devious, evil, intentional or ruthless our transgressions are. How can we say we love our sisters and brothers if we refuse to forgive them? When we were yet sinners, daily opposing and rebelling against the love and will of God, He yet demonstrated His love for us by taking on our sins (the very nature that he hated about us) and dying a painful death just for our benefit. Now I ask, what has anyone done to you that is so bad, so hurtful and so undesirable that you would allow it to separate you from your opportunity to demonstrate your Father's likeness? I, like anyone else, have been rejected, lied on, misrepresented, talked about, deceived, abandoned, hurt, disappointed and anything else you can imagine that could happen to a person. Yet, I go on record today as publically stating that it doesn't matter who did those things to me, why they did them or how they would ever have the audacity to do them, today I want the world and every demon in hell, every ruler of darkness and evil in high places to know that regardless of what anyone has ever done to me, I totally and fully forgive them.

I'm not asking you to do what I do unless I first demonstrate and live by own teaching. I would not dare to ask you to forgive while I myself and in a state of paralysis due to unforgiving. God has too much to offer and to give to us, but He won't release it into an unrepentant, revengeful, mean-spirited and hard-hearted person because he or she will only misuse and abuse it. Stop allowing the failures of others (who did not receive your acts of kindness, hospitality, and charity as such) to hold you in a place of spiritual retardation and non-productivity. Forgive and move on. You are not the only person to have to do so. Jesus had to. The apostles had to. John the Baptist had to. Members of the early church had to. Stephen had to. Joseph had to. Moses had to. And all others who have chosen Christ as their savior and role model will also had to pick up their painful cross and do the same. Many are the afflictions of the saints. Being hurt by those whom you attempt to help and abandoned by those whom you trust most is just one such affliction. Let go of it. Let it go. It has not helped or progressed you to this point in your life and chances are good that it will not progress or help you at any other point in your life. It is only a retardant, a detractor, a test. Push through it. You can do it, but only if you truly to will to do it. Set it free. Release it as a part of you that you give back to the atmosphere. Don't allow it to linger and control you. Rather, allow the love of God to rest, rule and abide within your heart. Pray a sincere prayer and ask God to take whatever it is that you are holding in your heart against ANYONE away and to replace it with the healing power of His love and peace. Then call that person and speak words of kindness, hope and prosperity over their life. You have the power to bind the adversary; why, then, would you allow Him to bind and steal, kill and destroy your God likeness? It's only one step, but this single step can catapult you miles along your path of your spiritual walk with

God. "FORGIVE US THIS DAY OF OUR TRANSGRESSIONS AS WE FORGIVE OUR THOSE WHO HAVE TRESPASSED AGAINST US." I love you too much, Dear God, not to do all that I can to be like You. Forgiving is one thing I can do . . . even if it hurts. After all, in the end it heals much more than it hurts.

Blessings.

A PAUSE FOR PRAYER

God, if I were perfect there would be no need for this prayer. I pray it because I am fully aware that like all other flesh and blood people, I too have missed the mark and have fallen short. Whether I have done so intentionally, in error, out of ignorance, or whatever, I confess that I have demonstrated behavior which does not line up with Your teachings, Your statues or Your character. Therefore, God, I have transgressed You and Your goodness and Your mercies. Thus, the need for me to humbly come before you to seek Your forgiveness and Your love. But, God, how can I do so if I am unwilling and unable to share this same love with those who transgress against me? How hypocritical would I be to send up a petition of forgiveness to You on my own behalf and then to harden my heart into a state of unforgiving against those who have committed like transgressions against me? Holy Spirit, I yield this vessel that You may love through me in spite of me. I pray that You will demonstrate unfeigned charity to those whom I would have harbored anger against and that You will bring me into unity and love with those I would have ostracized. I pray that You will command, control and communicate through this yielded vessel, and that every iota of hatred, vengefulness, selfishness, retaliation and divisiveness be subdued, overcome, arrested and totally spiritually debilitated within me. Purge me with the pleasant aroma of forgiveness. Correct and council me with the languages of love and forgiveness. I pray that this vessel will receive and operate in Your agape love and with feet shod with the preparation of peace, will take it along with the power of the Gospel into every crevice of the world that men might see You through and in me and will ask, "What must I do to be saved?" And all, God, because I have loved. In Jesus name, Amen.

Our Prayer

God, I pray that this day be the day that I love You least for the rest of my life. I pray that my love for You will grow bountifully with the coming and going of each new day. And because I cannot love You more until I love more those whom I see each day, I begin this day by asking that You ". . . forgive me of my debts as I forgive my debtors." Forgive me of my trespasses, blunders, stumbles, mistakes, direct and intentional disobedience, prideful ways, and all other wrong doings just as I forgive those who have in any way wronged me. Forgive me of judging, but only as (to the same extent, in the same way, to the exact degree) as I forgive those who have judged me. Forgive my errors against You and Your ways, but only as I forgive those who have erred in some way as they have dealt with me. Forgive me for not always being there for You, but only as I forgive those who deserted, abandoned and cast me aside. Forgive me, Father, because I know I have not always been an ideal child, friend or called out on, but only to the extent that I have forgiven others who walk in these same shoes in our relationship. Forgive me selfishness, but only to the extent that I have forgiven those who have dealt selfishly with me. Forgive my stiff-neck, prideful and arrogant ways, but only as I have forgiven those who have behave as such toward me. Forgive my ignorance, but only as I have forgiven and attempted to teach the unenlightened. Forgive my misspoken words and my unrighteous deeds, but only as I have forgiven the lies and corrupted slanders of speakers in my own life. Let me BE the love, the miracle, the peace, the example of You that I so often seek to find in others. Let it begin here and now and with me. Let me have no excuses. Let me not permit un-forgiveness to cause me to abandon my calling or to walk in disobedience. Humble me beneath Your mighty hand that I may hear from You, commune with You and cooperate with Your will and plan for my life in all that I do. Forgive my frailties and vulnerabilities as I have forgiven these human weaknesses in others. Forgive my human prejudices as I have forgiven those who have been, and even are, prejudice against me. I am the salt of the earth. But if I lose my saltiness, of what kingdom good am I? I recognize that I must forgive in order to love, in order to be in Your likeness, in order to walk in obedience, in order to be Your child. And, so, God, I choose not to walk according to my own history, my own emotions, my own experiences, or my own understanding, but, rather, according to Your will, Your statues and Your word which says ". . . by this shall the world know that ye are My disciples indeed, that ye love ye one another." Blessed be Your name, forever praised are Your ways and eternal is Your word. Blessed is my spirit to receive the words of this prayer today. Amen and amen.

Blessings.

Procrastination Is Only A Euphemism for Refusal

Hesitation and indecisiveness will only leave
you in your current position longer

Why We Can't Wait

Several years ago, the esteemed Rev. (Dr.) Martin Luther King, Jr. wrote from his jail cell in Birmingham, Alabama a soul stirring, spirit touching and morality provoking letter entitled "Letter from a Birmingham Jail". It has since stood the test of time and is today regarded as one of the most significant and powerful speeches given by this exemplary rhetorician. By no means is it the historical importance of this piece alone which makes it so memorable and such a treasure to all of us who identify and relate to the logos, pathos and ethos of such a great persona. But equally as important is how eloquently and lucidly he undertook and achieved the daunting task of laying out such a meticulous argument. His argument was so cogent that not even his enemies dared not to voice an opposing position. What a representative for his cause. What a warrior to have in the foxhole alongside you.

Dr. King ensured that no meaningful counter argument could ever stand against his assertions as he began to anticipate and strategically disarm other possible arguments. He did this several times during the course of his writing, but two times in particular stand out in my mind, and these were when by way of this epistle, he responded to the following criticisms cloaked as inquiries: 1) Why are you here? 2) Why can't the Negro wait (a little longer for his justice to come)? Dr. King answered the first question with the piercingly simply retort, "I am here because injustice is here. And injustice anywhere is a threat to justice everywhere." And to the latter, he replied by providing a litany of evidences (which would later be transformed into proofs) by reminding those who criticized him that justice too long delayed is justice denied and that it is easy for those who have never felt the dart-like stings of segregation to advance the notion of "wait". It is easy for those whose mothers and sisters are not being raped and whose fathers and sons, no matter their ages, share the same first name always—boy—to support the notion of "wait". It is not hard to see the logic in "waiting" if it isn't your children who are being denied access to the city parks and into restaurants and hotels because their skin is dark. You can say "wait" when you are the employer, but "wait" doesn't have the same melodious ring when it falls onto the ear of your unemployed brother, sister, or cousin who is already living beneath the poverty line.

"Wait," Dr. King explained, usually is better and more accurately defined as "never" because those who are empowered rarely—if ever—willingly surrender their power to those who are without power. And so, Dr. King went on to explain, "Just as the prophets of the 8th century B.C. left their villages and carried 'thus said the Lord' far beyond the boundaries of their home towns, and just as the Apostle Paul left his village of Tarsus and carried the gospel of Jesus Christ to the far corners of the Greco-Roman world, so am I compelled to carry the gospel of freedom beyond my own home town. Like Paul, I must constantly respond to the Macedonian call for aid, [because] there are two kinds of laws. There is a just law which every individual has a moral duty and responsibility to obey. And there is an unjust law which every person has a legal and moral duty to disobey, for an unjust law is not a law at all," but a form of robbery and deprivation.

And so here we are Christians. Here we are believers. Here we are disciples of Christ. Are we, like Dr. King, also compelled to take our gospel forth into the world or have we decided that there is no use in doing so anymore? Dr. King was very steadfast and bold in his claim as to his purpose. Even in jail and at the point of criticism from many of his fellow (white) clergy, he never relented. He said, "I am here because injustice is here. And injustice anywhere is a threat to justice everywhere." Why, then, does God have you here. If He no purpose for your presence here why didn't He save you and rapture you out of here? Could it be because YOU STILL HAVE A DIVINE PURPOSE HERE? Why are you here? Why? Did God save you just for you or did He save you so that YOU could be the salt of the earth and allow men to see you worship your Father who is in heaven and glorify Him? Could that be? Why are we here? WE ARE HERE BECAUSE SIN IS HERE!! AND IF INDIVIDUALS ARE GOING TO BE LEAD AWAY FROM SIN IT WILL BE AS A RESULT OF <u>US</u> PREACHING, AND <u>US</u> TEACHING, AND <u>US</u> PRAYING AND <u>US</u> TESTIFYING AND <u>US</u> FASTING AND <u>US</u> LIVING FOR CHRIST. WE ARE STILL HERE BECAUSE <u>WE ARE HIS REPRESENTATIVES</u>!!!

What could be worse than having someone represent you and they don't even know they're your representative!! How can they carry out their duties (obey)? How can they establish quality communication (prayer)? How can they compel others of your laws and statues (teach)? How can they persuade others of your policies (preach)? How can they model your wisdom, glory and power (let their light so shine)? How can they successfully carry out the mission you have released them to execute (allow You, Your presence and Your power to operate through them)? How? How can they if they have no idea why they're here?

If there were no sin in the earth then God would not need any saints here either. If there were no patients, would we need doctors? If there were no law breakers, would we need policemen? If there were no sin, why would there be a need for Christians on earth? I ask you again, why are you here? Do you know?

Why are you waiting? Every day you wait, you can believe it when I tell you, another soul has lost a chance to be that prodigal child who is now returned home. As Dr. King so beautifully and powerfully stated it, wait can often be defined as never. No, not that the chance for you to do what you were sent here "never" came about, but that you simply "NEVER" took advantage of it and spoke into somebody's life. Can you imagine if you could peer down into the depth of hell and into the pain-filled eyes of a lost soul and think to yourself, "S/he's there—for eternity—because I never spoke the Word of God into his spirit." What a travesty!!

I admit, our sisters and mothers are not being raped; and our men are now being recognized by their given names. But I also recognize that we cannot become complacent with this social advancement while spiritually nearly as many men are sleeping with other men as there are men sleeping with women. And women, likewise, are opting to become bed warmers for one another. Today in our country there are nearly as many people sold out to crack, alcohol, and other mood altering drugs as there are Christians. Destroying young babies in the womb has become as common place as casual sex and violence is being marketed to our families from ages pre-k through adulthood. This is why we can't WAIT. We can't wait for homosexuality to become the normal representation of family life in our country and we certainly can't wait for the anti-Christian movements to lobby all of our Christian rights away before we begin to speak up! We can't pray in schools, but we can hand out contraceptives! We can't pray or teach Christ, but we can teach tolerance! We can't discipline our children, but we can visit them in the jails! Why are we here? And what are we doing about it?

It is an injustice for us to allow God's people anywhere to perish because of our inactivity. The devil has worked well through his vessels in order to lobby for, write and pass a number of unjust laws (laws that do not stand up to the scrutiny or application of the Word of God), and we, Christians, have sat back, closed our mouths and decided to WAIT while the Kingdom of God is being robbed.

Does anyone else feel compelled to spread the Word of God? I'm not asking how do you feel physically? I'm not asking how's your financial status or anything of that nature. I'm simply asking does it bother you that the devil is deceiving our young people, destroying our marriages, releasing new diseases every day, confusing minds, destroying morality, infusing violence and seemingly just having his way here on the earth? Despite these depressing facts, God has decreed that man yet has dominion over his entire creation! Further, He reminded us that ". . . the prayers of a righteous man availeth much." So let's make this very simple and Word-backed. If you know that you know that you are saved, then do this. Point to yourself and say, "I am the righteousness of God. Which means I am righteous. Which further means that MY prayers availeth, bring about or cause much to manifest!"

How long do we stand around, power-filled and glory-endowed and yet let the devil have his way with God's property? That's like two grown parents allowing a two year old to run their house!

You're here because you have a mission, purpose and power here. This is your appointed place and assignment at this point in time. You can't wait because according to the Word of God, ". . . hell enlarges itself daily" in order to accommodate her ever increasing numbers. Our counterpart—the deceiver—never WAITS. He doesn't take days off, complain about bad days, go on vacation, take sick leave or waste his diabolic talents sitting around starring at a television screen. He's always SEEKING (NOTE: that's an active word) whom he may DEVOUR! Will the next person he devours be one whom YOU failed to share the gospel with? Believers, we must teach, preach and live God's truth as it is the only balm that can cure the human spirit of its deepest ills. We cannot permit shame, pride, doubt or anything other than faith and confidence in God and his unwavering, everlasting word to control us. We must love not the world or anything that is in the world, for to the extent that we love the world, it is to that same extend that we hate our God.

We cannot serve both God and Mannon. But if you would only make up your mind, I promise you, you can serve God our Lord and Savior and He will bless you like you could never have asked, thought, imagined or believe. Now please—be about your Father's business. In other words, don't wait any longer. Get to work NOW! Blessings!

Follow the wisdom of God,
Not the knowledge of man

Trust in the Lord with all your heart and lean not to
your own understanding but acknowledge the Lord
in all your ways and He will direct your path

Allow the Spirit of God to Interrupt Your Ignorance

Someone once said to me that the single most powerful teaching of Christ was the B Attitudes as recorded in Matthew, Chapter 5, verses 3-12 from Jesus' Sermon on the Mount message. I do believe that the Blessed Attitude teachings and verses are very powerful, personally, I love the second part of the message that Christ taught in that same chapter. The Blessed Attitude is what we must display, but often there are so many blocks to us getting to the attitude and one of the most frequently tripped over obstacle in our path is not the devil or trials or other people. Often it is trying to get past the erroneous teachings that we have been subjected to all of our (spiritual) lives. We have been taught doctrine that does not line up with the Word of God. We have been given advice that is not Godly council. We have been enlightened unto the knowledge of "learned men" but not unto the wisdom of God by anointed or God-sent men. As a result, we now seek to configure that which is absolute (TRUTH) to coincide with our own imaginings and have placed our trust in what we can see, touch, taste, feel, wear, drive, reside in, or consume. Thus are the origins of our own traditions, which, of course, make the word of God of no effect in our lives. Thus is the rise of "other Gods" in our hearts, though we profess and confess that "Thou shall have no other God before me." Thus is the rise of options that lead us astray and into temptation and away from the narrow path. That is why I believe that the second half of this teaching is awesome and very personal. For anyone who can live according to the dictates of the latter verses can in fact, sincerely display not only the fruit of the Spirit but the B Attitude as well. Let's see why.

God (Jesus in the flesh) is the His own Word. Many "religious" groups, by the time Jesus came, had devised their own teachings, code, laws, behaviors, religious expectations and the like. As a result, "saints" had begun to keep the teachings of their churches (man-made salvation) and their religions and their traditions, but had strayed from the strict and Holy teachings of God. This is one of the reasons that the Jews had such a hard time accepting the teachings of Christ, because the teachings of THE TRUTH directly conflicted with the religious teachings of man. The Jews believed so strongly in THEIR laws and rituals and practices that when THE TRUTH arrived and spoke directly to them they argued, rebelled, rejected and resented Him to the point of crucifixion. (It is a sad commentary when you live your entire life to dwell with truth, yet you don't even recognize truth when He walks and talks with your daily.)

Christ starts us off in verse twenty by straightforwardly informing us ". . . **That except your righteousness shall exceed the righteousness of the scribes and Pharisees, ye shall in no case enter into the kingdom of heaven**". But why? Why did he say this before he went into the second half of one of His most powerful teachings delivered to those who wished to become His disciple? A little more reading will reveal the answer.

In verse 21 Jesus begins with these words: "Ye have heard that it was said by them of old . . . ." In other words He was telling them that the mis-teachings of those who previously instructed you have, taught you that THIS is the way you are to behave in this given situation. But instantly (Verse 22) Jesus comes back and corrects the erroneous teachings that have been misleading his people. He does this by starting the verse off with the word "BUT". But is a perfect word to use here as the word "but" acknowledges a contradiction and a departure from the previous. Therefore (verse 21) "[previously] Ye have heard that it was said by them of old . . ." BUT now comes the contradiction. Now the TRUTH speaks and removes the erroneous teachings that have guided us not TO but away from Him. He says, (verse 22) "But I (the TRUTH, the way, God in the flesh, the perfect and inerrant Word manifested in flesh) . . . I SAY . . ." Yep. God, in the form of Jesus stepped onto the scene and corrected the corrupted word. But He didn't stop there. He went further.

In verse 27 He takes us back to the mis-information we have been fed all of our spiritual lives. Again He starts us off with the same words, "Ye have heard that it was said by them of old time . . . ." However, He comes right back and uses the same terminology to re-direct our errant understanding unto His true path of righteousness. What does He say in verse 28? You got it! "But I say unto you . . . ." Yep, the old teachers said A, but here comes God in the flesh and tells us B. How great He is! But He still doesn't stop here either.

In verse 31 He again tells us that "It hath been said [taught, instilled,]"; nonetheless, He who would not have us deceived by the wiles of the evil one (mis-teaching is a wile, by the way), comes right back again in verse 32 and clears the fog from the minds of our spirits by telling us "But I say . . . ." In other words, let me interrupt your ignorance and put an end to all of this mis-teaching.

Now this would be enough if Jesus stopped here, but you know what? He didn't. Look at verses 33 and 34. First He identifies the mis-information in verse 33 ("Again ye have heard that it has been said by them of old . . .") and then He corrects it in verse 34 by letting us know the TRUTH on the matter, "But I say unto you . . . ."

In verse 37 He digresses and quickly takes the time to teach us of the Christian necessity of governing what comes out of our mouths, then He returns (verse 38-44) to again teach us the truth about what we've been mis-taught. In verse 37, true to form, He again says to us "Ye have heard that it hath been said . . . ." But this time He leaves the though open until He reaches verse 45. Here He makes it perfectly clear as to why He has been correcting all of the mis-teachings which have resulted in so many mis-directed and lost souls.

He's not doing it because He wants to make our way hard or difficult. He's not doing it because He doesn't want us to enter into the Kingdom of God. He's not doing it because He's trying to discourage us. He does it simply "That ye may be the Children of your Father which is in heaven . . . ." (Remember: If you are not a child of God's 'You will **in no case** enter into the Kingdom'.") He testifies of that which He knows. He is the only way to the Father. We must believe Him if we are to ever belong to the Father. And so, the Father, in the form of the Son, who has been found in the form of a man, who is the Word Himself, has taken the time to leave His divine throne and to carefully, lovingly and meticulously teach us clearly and accurately the only path which leads unto eternity with Him.

Could this be why Jesus said to Nicodemus, "Nicodemus, art thou a teacher of the Jews and know ye not these things?" In other words, Nicodemus, you're a teacher. You're responsible for spreading the TRUTH of the gospel. How can you if you do not yourself know truth? You know traditions. You know laws. You know ordinances and you know intellect. But you are lacking in truth, and, thus, what you have learned and taught is errant and has caused many to perish for it is the knowledge of the TRUTH that sets one free and the lack thereof which keeps one in bondage.

In many of our churches today many of us have a need to ask, "Art thou a teacher of the people of God, and know ye not these things? Or do you teach me traditions and wait for God to say to me, "But I say . . ."?

Blessings.

A PAUSE FOR PRAYER

(A Prayer for the Feeble Among Us)

Father, bless the mind, the soul, the emotions and the faith of your children of every race, creed, color and nationality. Allow us all to dare to believe and to receive in the depth of our hearts Your divine promise that "nothing shall be impossible to those who believe" your every word. Allow us to rise early every morning and to lift the name of Jesus, Your only begotten Son and incarnated Word, in words of praise, exaltation, expectation and faith. Teach us, oh Spirit of purity, power and love, the powers that only that name can release in this realm. Give us enlightenment and understanding beyond that of our carnality. Allow us to bow our hearts and knees to You in humble submission, supplication and surrender, for it is not until we do this that You will be able to reveal Yourself, Your power and Your will to all of us.

Forgive us of all unrighteous thoughts, behaviors, and beliefs that are inconsistent with Your teachings and ways. Consume us, Holy Spirit, and create within us a clean heart and renew within us a righteous spirit. For the benefits of our faith are directly transferable to the situation which presently plagues our families, situations, and loved ones. Teach us, Holy Spirit, as no man can. Say the things directly into our spirit that only your spirit can say and in the only way that we can recognize and receive them as absolute truth. Comfort us, oh God, in the quietness of the night and the loneliness of the day, as only You can.

Give rest and peace unto our minds, our hearts and even our faith. Let us know that if we would simply confess You as our Lord and Savior that we will then have the benefit of coming before You—boldly—and asking for Your divine intervention into situations that no man can change, reverse, fix or impact. But, God, because of our faith, You will supernaturally work in the situation to bring about a miracle which will change the lives of many. Walk with us. Talk with us. Comfort us. Touch us where no natural hand can. Laugh with us through our tears and smile with us through our brief moments of fear.

Holy Spirit, let us know that You are our ever-present helper and that You are right there just waiting for us to surrender the battle and to take down our garment of faith. Let us decree that You and You alone are the only god who is fit for us to serve, to surrender to, to call our Lord and to turn our life, our heart and our eternity over to. Go with us now and let us know that this is Your will for us. And as an earthly intercessor, I pray this prayer as a warrior who stands in the gap for those who lack the faith and spiritual wisdom and commitment to receive its power and manifestations.

I stand here God that my faith will go before You as a surrogate until their faith has been developed to a level at which it can call those things which be not as though they are, and can do so in full righteous confidence. I command the angels which harken unto Your voice and are sent to minister (assist) believers in the carrying out of Your will in the earth realm, to be encamped round about them. Hedge them in. Protect them by the power of the One who sent you. We—the angels and I together—rebuke every attempt of the adversary to disrupt the joys and pleasures of their lives! Together, we bind every evil attempt of the adversary to deprive them and/or their families of joy, faith, and righteous confidence. And we release into their lives faith, strength, might, wisdom, insight and righteous boldness. Let them go forth now in faith and SPEAK everywhere their feet trod, the hope, the expectation and the deepest beliefs of what You have already done in their lives and in their situations.

And, God, let them walk, believe and speak by FAITH and not by sight. Give peace to their minds as they matriculate through life, as they will need You in order to remain the your Salt of the earth and Your light which sits upon a hill that cannot be hidden. Bring their studies of your Holy Word back to their memories and give them sweet, peaceful, fruitful and renewing rest each night. Sooth all of their pains, God, and speak words of confidence, compassion and assurance into their inner person every day. May Your grace and mercy be their constant companions. And not only theirs, Father, but everyone with whom they come in contact for the Kingdom sake.

Now, God, I release this prayer to You in confidence and in total faith as I know You are at work in their situations. And because it is Your greatest pleasure to give the best of heaven to us, Your earthly children, I say thank you, Daddy for what You have already done through the words of this prayers for all who have believed, received and prayed it. And so, we close this prayer with Your immutable words of faith which remind us that NO WEAPON FORMED AGAINST US SHALL PROSPER. It is so, because Your word is forever settled in heaven and will not return unto You void, but will accomplish that which You have sent it unto. And by way of your humble and yielded servant, as moved by Your Holy Spirit, Your word has been sent to destroy situations even unknown unto me that You and You alone may be glorified in all that Your humble servant says and do in Your name.

Father, I have in this prayer, prayed the words of my belief and I have prayed back unto You, the words of Your own promises to us, your children. We try you, Father, that the unbelievers may be convinced and convicted and converted and receive and believe You until they see You face to face and eternally. We confess and profess that the petitions of this supplication are answered and that everything asked for in this prayer is done. In Jesus name, we faithfully proclaim our victory . . . . Amen.

Blessings.

Study to shew yourself approved a workman
rightly dividing the Word of God . . . .

For God is not unjust so as to overlook your work and the love that
you have shown for His name in serving the saints, as you still do.

And he said unto them, How is it that ye sought me? Wist
ye not that I must be about my Father's business?

Put your hands to work for the kingdom

(Whatsoever thing you do, do it as unto the glory of God)

FEW LABORERS? MAYBE THIS IS WHY

People of God, I want to present you with a precious yet urgent charge today; and here it is. The Bible tells us to know those who labor among us. Often we take this scripture to only mean to know their gifting, their talents and their anointing. But the word "know" here means to be intimately involved with them. It means to be aware of more than the name of their favorite song, or what office they occupy in church or even where they live. It also refers to knowing their struggles, being familiar with their pains, understanding their moods. It means talking with them even when they are not very friendly in return. It means holding them and crying with them just because you sincerely care that much about them. It means listening with the intent to help and not to gossip. It means sharing a part of yourself so that they know they are not unique in their current dilemma.

Saints, there are a lot of Christians who are walking around among us who are one argument from a divorce, one pay check from bankruptcy, one more incident from "losing it," one more trial from giving up and one more rejection from taking their own life. They're not a distance away. They're not across the street or down the road in somebody else's church. They're not even in another family or a neighbor in somebody else's neighborhood. They're the same people who are smiling at you. They're the same people who are trying to press their way through tears, fears and trials. They're your co-workers, next door neighbors, pastors, friends, colleagues and others whom you'd never suspect or expect. But so often we're never aware, or in other words, we don't know those who labor among us, because we are so busy laboring and wallowing in our own situations and self-pity that we swear that we just don't have the time or energy to entertain anyone else's.

Well, today I want to charge every believer to make it a point to do this: (Early in the morning will I seek your face.)

1. Get up at least 30 minutes earlier than you usually do.
2. TOTALLY devote these 30 minutes (or so) to Christ in fervent prayer.
3. Give yourself over to the Father that He may fully occupy, use and control you as He wishes.
4. Express your intent and desire to be a conduit for Him, His Voice and His power ALL DAY TODAY.
5. Ask God to lead and guide your every action and step. Then ask Him to lead you to hurting individuals that He may use your vessel to speak through, to heal through, to restore through and to redeem through.
6. Go into your kitchen and get a drink (juice preferably) and bread or cracker. Administer communion to yourself and understand that when you "commune with" you become as one with.
7. Allow yourself to be lead by the Spirit of God. When He leads you to a brother or sister, go to them and tell them very honestly, that you have done the above steps and that the Spirit of God has unctioned you to pray with/for them.
8. Ask them if there is anything in particular they would like to talk with you about or if there is something going on in their life for which they want prayer.
9. And if they receive you, allow the Holy Spirit to pray through you, but first make sure you let them know that a

prayer that is not traveling on the wings of faith is a prayer that is not likely to leave the earth realm.

10. Allow the Holy Spirit to prayer for them through you then if they are willing, exchange contact info just in case they "decide" there is something they want to prayer about later. Bless them and repeat the process.

For those who are saying, I'm not going up to a complete stranger and . . . . whatever. Just remember that God can't use cowards or rebellious children. Hopefully He can use YOU though.

There are a lot of people who are right among us who are hurting. A lot of them won't be in a prayer line on Sunday simply because if you don't get to them during the week, they won't be in anybody's church this or any other Sunday—until they are rolled in by a mortician.

We are a unique people. There are not many of us. Please, let us be as iron sharpening iron. Let those of us of the household of faith look after those of us after the household of faith. Don't be afraid to be anointed or used. Don't hesitate. Don't doubt. When you are yielded, it is no longer you who live, but Christ who lives and operates in and through you on behalf of the Father. I leave you with the thought of Marianne Williamson as it is most fitting for this teaching:

Our Deepest Fear

"**Our deepest fear is not that we are inadequate. Our deepest fear is that we are powerful beyond measure. It is our light, not our darkness that most frightens us. We ask ourselves, 'Who am I to be brilliant, gorgeous, talented, fabulous?' Actually, who are you NOT to be? You are a child of God. Your playing small does not serve the world. There is nothing enlightened about shrinking so that other people won't feel insecure around you. We are all meant to shine, as children do. We were born to make manifest the glory of God** that is within us. It's not just in some of us; it's in everyone (of us). And as we let our own light shine, we unconsciously give other people permissions to do the same. As we are liberated from our own fears, our presence automatically liberates others." (Maryann Williamson)

For one day, ignore your own needs, pains, desires and petitions and take the time to dedicate this day to helping a stranger who by the grace of God may be called into or restored unto the works of the Kingdom.

Know ye not that it is time for us to be about our Father's business? If you love Him, feed His sheep.

Blessings.

Let your light so shine that men may see your good
works and glorify your Father which is in Heaven.

For God is not unjust so as to overlook your work and the love that
you have shown for His name in serving the saints, as you still do.

And he said unto them, How is it that ye sought me? Wist
ye not that I must be about my Father's business?

**(Remember to live your life in such a way
that it merits a repeat performance.)**

BRAVO! MORE! BRAVO!

Being a playwright and actor, I know personally that there is
nothing more precious to us than to hear our audience applaud our
performance and scream the words "Bravo! Bravo! More! More!"

What these simple words say to the heart of an actor and writer
is that your message, your artistic worth, your ambition, your goal
has been achieved in this particular undertaking and that your
performance has moved beyond just the boundaries of your creative
skills and has impacted your viewers at a much deeper level. You
have left an artistic impression on the psyche, soul, spirit and words
of all who have seen and experienced your work. Never again can
you take singular credit for your laudable performance, but it now
becomes entwined and co-owned by everyone who saw it as well
as everyone who contributed to its success. This includes the co-
writers (who saw the vision before others saw the performance),
the musicians (who created a musical atmosphere upon and within
which the performance was strategically encased), the producers
(who saw to it that you had everything required to bring your
vision in full fruition), the director(s) (who took the written words
off the page and gave them life and meaning), the actors (who used
their creative talents and skills to give actual personage to fictional
characters), the ticket salesmen (who distributed "passes" to the
performance), the ushers who assisted "mis-directed patrons find
the seats indicated on their "passes"), the stage and house managers
who assumed responsibilities for all that goes in the theater or

on/behind the stage, the "techies" (who ensures that the sound, the lighting and all of the technical aspects of the production are carried out to perfection). And many, many others.

Likewise are our lives. As Shakespeare has said, all life is a production and all mankind is its cast. The big question here, however, is not whether or not you're an actor, a musician, a technician or a skill-level person. Rather, the big question is what quality will your performance, known as your life, be remembered as? Will your audience rise to its anxious feet and cheer your performance while happily wishing for "more" and shouting "bravo!"? Or will the curtains fall on your final act to an empty house with no one caring how the finale of your production concludes?

Will your performance (life) have served someone other than yourself? Will it have changed somebody else's production (path) as well. Or when the credits are given will everyone of them be identified as "I"? I wrote. I acted. I directed. I organized. I contributed. I produced. I danced. I sang. I did it all, and as a result, what "I" have done is to put on a one person show that has not impacted, influenced, changed, or given direction to anyone else except myself.

Can you imagine that? I've lived a long, full, successful life, yet I have not impacted one alcoholic. I have not counseled with one troubled soul. I have not up-lifted one down-trodden spirit. I have not encouraged one doubtful mind. I have not made any personal sacrifices so that someone else can achieve their dream. I have not lead one sinner into prayer. I have no encouraged anyone, except when it behooved me and gave public visibility to my behavior. I have not shared my wisdom with the unlearned nor my hope with the faithless. I have not given to the poor except that the masses might know my deeds and give praise to me. I have not fed the hungry nor given the bread of life to the spiritually starving. I. I. I. What a wretch "I" am inspite of my achievements!

If I have not done these things, why should there be chants of "Bravo" and "More" when the curtain falls on my performance (life)? Why would anyone chant for more selfishness, more individual pride, more egotism, more self-serving, more unforgiving and less godlessness?

Our lives have become such an influx of materiality and personal acquisitions, that we often forget that no matter how many or how much we amass, ultimately, we must and will die and leave it. We will leave this realm as empty of its possessions as we entered it. The gold will be left behind, likely in the same jewelry boxes as the diamonds. The beautiful dwellings will remain here as well and will be exchanged for a coffin. The extensive and costly wardrobes will remain under the care and will be managed by decisions of those who are unable to wear its offerings and will likely give it to those whom many of us failed to bless during our performance (lives).

My brothers and sisters believe the words of truth which teach us that only what you do for Christ will last. Our rewards are stored up in heaven where thieves CANNOT break in and the moths and the rust CANNOT destroy. Our lives are but our service opportunity to God's prime creation—mankind. What good is it to know about love if we don't share love? What good is it to have if we do not bless others? What good is knowing if we permit our brothers and sisters to continue to operate in ignorance? And why should we expect those whom we have abandoned and ignored to recognize the godlikeness in us and to applaud and desire it, if we never took the time to "let our light so shine" into their dying and crumbling world and souls?

When all my days are over and done and I have answered the call of both burden and fun

Will I be able to say in my heart, "I know a good race for the Kingdom I truly have run?"

When all my days are over and done and I can no longer impact the young on their final outcome

Will I hear my Savior's sacred decree, "Well done my good and faithful one. Well done"?

When all my days are over and done and I can longer admire God's setting sun

Will I meet Jesus in Paradise with my new life having just begun?

When all my days are over and done and I must rest and forevermore hold my tongue

Will I then sing in the angelic choir or maybe beat the heavenly drums?

When all my days are over and done will heaven hold for me countless rewards or none?

Will Jesus know me not and reject me face to face or will he thank me for the race I've run?

Bravo? More? You be the judge . . . before Christ does. And any place you find that your presentation is weak—ensure to eliminate that deficiency. For the cries of bravo and more come from a discerning audience only when the initial performance is one of the best they've ever seen.

Blessings.

Thou shall also decree a thing and it shall be established unto thee

Let the weak say I am strong!

I would therefore that men pray everywhere, lifting
up holy hands, without wrath and doubting not

An Inspired Declaration of War

Have you ever seen a fierce competitor get right to the finish line then give up or give out because his or her conditioning was not sufficient to take them to the end of the race? I have. I've seen some runners lead their races from the starting gun until seconds from crossing the finish line. How can this be? How can they endure 99% of the race and then give out in the final 1%? How? Because the race is not given to the swift or the strong, but to him who endureth TO THE END. Conditioning yourself to run 99% of a race is the same as conditioning yourself to lose the race and to fail. The only difference is that your failure comes later in the race rather than sooner. Yet, failure will be that runner's ultimate outcome.

Likewise, why run this Christian race 99% of the way and fall short in the final home stretch? Surely none of us knows when the final home stretch is for us as Christians, therefore, we condition ourselves to run and to endure until we hear the buzzer going off, which for us is the voice of God saying "Well done my good and faithful servant. Well done. In YOU I am highly pleased."

To whom it may concern. Don't give up. The reward is too great. The truth of the promises are too certain. The hope is too real. And the reward for second place (quitting on Christ) isn't quite like the silver medal stand at the Olympic Games. Much may have gone wrong in your life, but don't quit. Many may have spoken falsely and even ridiculed you, but don't quit. You may have to soak your pillow at night and force a smile by day, but Saints of God, hang in there. If you have to hang in there alone, so be it. If you have to encourage yourself in the Lord as David did, (as Nike would say) just do it. If there is not a choir around you, sing by yourself and know that the angels in heaven are harmonizing with you—BUT DON'T YOU QUIT!! Don't do it. If those in whom you had high regards have deserted you and have left you on this journey all alone, just know that your Savior will never leave or forsake you. So why would you quit—on HIM? But what if you don't have much at all? Continue the race with the little that you have knowing that if He could make two fish and five loaves of bread do what they did—and have leftovers—then certainly he can take your little, bless it, multiply it, extend it and ordain it to do exceedingly abundantly and above all that you could ever ask or think. So, please, don't quit. If your body is under attack, bring it under pray and under consecration and under dedication and under submission, but keep running this faith race. No mother? Then run for the motherless. No father? Then run for the fatherless. No family? Then run for those who yet need to be adopted into the family of Christ. Been hurt? Run that those who see you will learn the art of forgiving. Diminished hope? Run that those who have never known hope will see your zeal for Christ and become your running mates. Is the brilliance of your gospel light growing dim? Run that He may re-charge you with each step and that those who are yet in the kingdom of darkness may see your light and choose to follow after it.

Saints we cannot quite this race. For if we quite this race homosexuality, murder, lying, deception, corruptness, ungodly ways and ignorance to the laws and will of God will enter the race, pervert it and declare themselves lawful entrees as legal replacements for those who have quit. If this Christian battle depended upon your effort to either earn victory or suffer defeat, what could heaven count on you to do in this fight—right now??

Fight or flee? Will you be a warrior or a coward? Will you faint or will you endure? Will you make an excuse or give God a sacrifice?

There is a shifting that is about to take place. It's going to shake up some things that we never thought would we touched. It's going to align certain forces and seek to un-align others. Enemies will become allies and allies will become enemies. Ignorance will be taken as wisdom and wisdom will be dismissed for ignorance. Morality will be attacked and utterly morphed then eventually destroyed while immorality will be given free reign and will be encouraged and taught as the appropriate and desired thing after which to seek. Those who have had much will become poor and the poor of God shall have the riches of the earth lavished upon and into their lives. During this period THE CHURCH cannot identify herself along the lines of denominations. For only one "denomination" shall stand this test and that is the "denomination" of HOLINESS and holiness alone. Surely those who survive it shall be those who feast daily upon the bread of the word. Every warrior must have his weapons weapon (mouth and heart) locked and loaded with his only ammunition—the word of God. All solders must be properly combat uniformed at all times—that is the full armor of God. And there will be neither occasion, reason or time for idle words. For a time is coming when every word spoken shall be of kingdom purpose and with destiny manifestation.

If you are not in shape—get there! Start running your laps through the course of the Bible. Start pushing up prayers out of your spirit. Start chinning up to every challenge the evil one throws at you. Shine your armor and inspect it for cracks, dents, weak spots and compromising openings. Check your gospel vocabulary so that no corrupt communication proceeds out of your mouth. Slip on your (helmet) headgear just to be sure that when the battle gets heated you know who is charge of your thoughts in that way things that are pure and holy and righteous and of good report, you will think on them and every thought that is not like this you will bring into the captivity of the Holy Ghost. Try on your chest protector—it protects ALL of your vital organs, most importantly your heart. And be sure your feet are perfectly fitted in comfortable gospel carrying shoes. (Too many saints are on the sidelines right now simply because their feet (place of assignment) were uncomfortable!)

This is more than a pointless writing. This is a warning to all of those who will hear it, believe it and heed it. There is a tremendous shake up about to hit the atmosphere and every one of us who is not in the best spiritual shape of our lives are going to either repel hell or catch hell. What's your condition saying right now? If it's not at its peak, I would advise you to get in the spiritual gym (presence of God) and bench press (press toward the mark of the higher calling) until you reach fatigue (the throne).

Ladies and gentlemen, there's a battle brewing. It's coming. It's powerful. It's long lasting. And it ain't gonna be no joke either. If you aren't ready, all I can tell you is . . . IN CADENCE!!! EXERCISE!!! 1 . . . 2 . . . 3 . . . 4! 1 . . . 2 . . . 3 . . . 4! 1 . . . 2 . . . 3 . . . 4!

Blessings. (Because we're going to need them more now than we have ever before!)

**God does not call the qualified;
God qualifies the called.**

Seasoning Verses Reasoning

A good reason can be found to support or refute nearly anything that we either want to support or wish to oppose. Reasoning is powerful. It is compelling. It is convincing. And, of course, because reasoning is often substantiated by empirical evidence, it is then difficult to discount—without appearing argumentative, unlearned or perhaps even recalcitrant.

But how will a believer ever come to realize who he is if he doesn't oppose the reasoning of the mind? How will a mere mortal man ever come to realize that he is more than the product of his mother's and father's base interactions if he never challenges or refute the presentations of logic? How will an infirmed person ever believe that by the stripes of Jesus Christ on Calvary cross, I am healed, whole and complete if he trusts what his eyes see and his mind comprehends? It won't happen. And it won't happen because all human reasoning will simply convince the natural man that his spiritual thinking is simply unreasonable, beyond reality and beyond the realm of truth. This is how reasoning works. And to place one's faith or trust in anything else simply escapes all human think and logic!

However, isn't it ironic how the promises of God all forego reasoning and seek to become a part of our lives through our faith? God's words, God's promises, God's power, God's privileges, God's salvation, God's love and all else God has for me is not and never has been predicated on my ability to reason it into manifestation. It is all made available to me on the basis of my faith in every word of God's promises to me. If I permit my reasoning to come into play, my reasoning will eventually and invariably destroy my faith because the deeds of faith are not subject to reason and can never be understood by reason. Consider the following examples: The word of God tells me of all the greatness that is within me and all of the mighty deeds and acts I am capable of manifesting if I would only believe in Him. But if I ran this promise through the mill of human reasoning, I would never be able to receive it as absolute truth because there are too many tangibles and intangibles that could logically make for a reasonable rebuttal. The Word tells me that I am more than a conqueror through Christ Jesus and that no weapon that is formed against me shall prosper. Trust me when I tell you, this is not an easy concept for the human mind to grasp. God will never leave me or forsake, but will supply my every need according to His exceeding riches in glory. Can a logical retort be made to this assertion? Logically speaking, yes. Faithfully speaking, no! How easy is it for a former prostitute or drug dealer to logically lay claim to the promise that God has decreed that I am the salt (seasoning) of the earth and I am His workmanship created unto good works before the foundation of the earth? How easy? Not easy—at all—unless the converted soul has accepted these promises by faith as absolute truth from God. This is one reason many believers often say something like I know this is the Word, but I don't know how this can be so in my life because "logically" when I think about all of the promises of God, it just doesn't make sense (or sound reasoning) how all of this could be a reality in my life. Well allow me to explain it in very simple terminology.

The reason that the spiritual promises of God make no sense to them is simply because they are not suppose to make "sense;" they are suppose to make faith. God never asked us to fight the good fight of "sense" and He, Himself, is not the "Sense-ful" one. Instead He told us to fight the good fight of faith and He Himself is the faithful one who hastens to perform His own word. God has spoken to us about a spiritual mystery which cannot be grasped or comprehended by the natural mind. It can only be laid hold of by faith in every word that He has spoken into our hearts.

Reasoning is a good thing, in an environment where reasoning is appropriate. However, it can be a murderous thing when it is erroneously misapplied to in environments where it is best left unapplied. Reasoning, to an extent, does apply to the things and Word of God. Do not be deceived that it does not. For even God Himself says, "Come, let us **reason** together." Why does He say this? Not to deny the existence of the empirical, but to use the empirical to confirm the existence of that which cannot be empiricalized, or in other words, the supernatural or spiritual.

God knows that the stars, galaxies and universes exist and all that is in them. Surely He does. He made them all and by Him were all things made. This includes ALL THINGS in heaven, upon the earth and in the earth to include powers, principalities, dominions and sub-microscopic particles. So empirical science is not something He wishes to debate in the spirit of man. Rather, what God wishes to do is to clearly show (**reason** with the naturally learned mind) how that which is seen testifies and confirms the existence of that which cannot be seen or experienced by way of senses.

True believers are who they are by way of **God's seasoning** and not man's reasoning. It is God who has seasoned your heart in such a way that the day you heard Him knock you did not harden your heart. Rather, you opened the door to your spirit and invited the Holy Ghost to take up residence inside of your spiritual man. And as a result, God sprinkled something on your heart called grace, mercy and forgive. He transformed you from the inside out. He changed you. He seasoned your spirit man and made it suitable for the palate of the Father's heart. He did not reason with you; He seasoned you.

It is said that Moses had the equivalent of over 20 doctorate degrees by today's educational standards—20 plus doctorates! Yet when God got ready to use him mightily, He sent him to the backside of the mountain and kept him back there all alone for

40 years. Why was that? What else was there for God to teach Moses? Moses knew languages, science, engineering, math, music, astronomy, economics, history, meteorology, leadership, architecture, literature and on and on. So with all of this accomplished "reasoning" why did God choose to leave Moses on the back side of the mountain for 40 years. Because he was "reasoned" but he was not yet "seasoned".

Had ANY MAN entered into a debate with Moses, no doubt Moses could have held his own and probably emerged as the victor. God knew this and so did Moses. So much so, that I believe Moses (at this time) had learned to rely and believe in his reasoning above his seasoning. Therefore, God had to take him on the back side of the mountain and empty him of all of his reasoning skills and replace them with the skills one can acquire only through the seasoning of God.

God began the reasoning verses seasoning process with Moses early on when Moses saw the burning bush which was never consumed by fire. Subsequently (Exodus 4:10) when God tells Moses of his assignment, Moses seeks to convince God (reason with Him) that he is not up to the assigned tasked. Look at what Moses says to God: Oh Lord, I am not eloquent, neither before now, nor since you have spoken to your servant; for I am SLOW of speech, and of a slow tongue." (Note it does not say he stuttered. He just was not one to think and respond quickly, and so he sought to use that as a justification of get out of his divine calling.)

But why would Moses say such a thing to God? Simple. He'd seen a burning/talking bush in the middle of the desert, yet the fire did not consume the dry bush. Though educated and well learned, Moses was unprepared to attempt to explain this phenomenon to anyone. For what could he say that would not make him appear foolish or unreasonable? How reasonable is it to explain that you saw a burning bush that was not consumed and out of it came a voice speaking to you? Is that reasonable? No. But if you had the experience, it's definitely seasoning.

What I believe Moses was telling God was I'm well learned, well educated, can reason exceptionally well, but when somebody asks me to explain my encounter with You, I'm lost for words. I can't articulate what I experienced without sounding like a fool. I can't make any wise person believe that You spoke to me through a burning bush yet the bush was not consumed. I can't rely on my education to do this for me because it has already and continues to fail me in this effort. I can't allow my religion to stand as my defense because there is no religion known to man that can validate such an experience. I can't let my background be my justification for what I experienced because there are too many more Hebrews who have never had such an experience. The truth is, I believe Moses argued, the more I try to explain it, the more foolish (or unreasonable) I sound! I'm going to be laughed to shame and ridiculed endlessly when I discuss this with men as learned (reasoned) as Pharaoh and his staff.

(And it must be noted that while the Bible never tells us that Moses actually stuttered, it clearly and definitely lets us know (in Acts 7:22) that "Moses was educated in all the wisdom of the Egyptians and was powerful in speech and action.")

So God had to separate Moses—for 40 years—in order to empty him of his reasoning, because the mission for which God had uniquely prepared Moses for was not one in which he could rely on his own intellectual reasoning skills. God was going to tell Moses to face a ruthless pharaoh, and he couldn't successfully do by human reasoning. He was going to take an unknown entity who had been hiding behind a mountain for the last 40 years of his life and make him the leader of an entire nation of people, and he couldn't do this by human reasoning. He was going to empower him to call plagues upon Egypt, but not by way of reasoning. He was going to cause Him to see God face-to-face, but not by reasoning. He was going to empower him to destroy the black magic of the pharaoh's magicians, but not by reasoning. He was going to tell him to lead him to a sea, with an army chasing after him and the Hebrew children and no way out. Then God was going to tell him to hold up the natural stick that was in his hand and watch the salvation and power of God do the rest. But he couldn't do this with reasoning. This could only be accomplished through spiritual seasoning.

And so God took him behind the mountain and prepared him. He purged him. He cleansed him. He strengthened him. He renewed him. He transformed form. He enlightened him. He taught. In a single word, God SEASONED him because God knew that where He wanted to take Moses and what He had for Moses to do, could not be reached or accomplished by way of reasoning. Reasoning versus seasoning.

But, please, don't leave the truth of this spiritual concept between God and Moses. This is one of the most powerful concepts in the Bible which also applies to each one of us. I cannot think of more accurate verses in the Bible to substantiate this claim than the verses found at Psalm 139:13-18:

13) For you formed my inmost being. You knit me together in my mother's womb.
14) I will give thanks to you, for I am fearfully and wonderfully made. Your works are wonderful. My soul knows that very well.
15) My frame wasn't hidden from you, when I was made in secret, woven together in the depths of the earth.
16) Your eyes saw my body (parts) in your book, they were all written, the days that were ordained for me, when as yet there were none of them.
17) How precious to me are your thoughts, God! How vast is their sum!
18) If I would count them, they are more in number than the sand. When I wake up, I am still with you.

From these verses a believer can plain see why he or she should never succumb to mere human reasoning. For instance, in verse 13 David explains that it was God who completely formed every aspect of his INNER being. He says that God did it while he was still in his mother's womb. This is very significant as David is trying to get us to see that it is not just his physical inner parts or being about which he is talking. David is saying, now that I know you, God, I realize that all of the greatness and divineness that lies within me, You and only You placed it there intentionally for a divine purpose while I was yet being formed inside my mother's womb. No man had a hand in the greatness that lies in me. I am YOUR handiwork, created to do wonderful things. What does this mean? You were seasoned before you were ever born! That's why God told Jeremiah that he knew him in the womb and ordained (seasoned him to be) him a prophet unto the nation. Do you not think this same God knew you in the womb too? Do you not believe He ordained and seasoned you as well? Or are you still trying to reason it?

In verse 14 David comes to understand the precision, purposefulness and perfection of God's plan and workmanship and he gives God praise for it. The eyes of his understanding are opened wide and he tells God, "I am fearfully and wonderfully made!" Why? Because he finally realized that he was made and seasoned for greatness before he ever left the womb. The only thing that had stopped him from walking in his seasoning was his natural reasoning.

Verse 15 David goes on to say that not one part of me was not designed, purposed, or ordained for anything short of greatness because not one ounce of him was left unseen, unexamined, or un-purposed by God.

Verse 16 David sees how perfect God is and how meticulous God plans and purposes. He says God actually has a book (owner's manual, if you will) with every part and its expiration date written in the divine operator's manual in heaven. He tells us that not only is every part numbered, but the length of every part's days are numbered even before the parts are assembled in a human body and released into the earth realm. (Everything about us has a divine purpose and mission. Moreover, everything about us has a divinely appointed lifespan as well.) Therefore, it becomes imperative that believers redeem the time and be about their Father's work. Every mission that you have been given by God to perform in this realm, you have also been seasoned to perform it. Don't let your reasoning convince you otherwise.

In verse 17 David examines, through his spiritual eyes the awesomeness of God and His plan, power and purpose and decrees that the thoughts of God toward His creation are so astounding that words are inadequate to express their majestic and empowering nature. He then goes on to allude to the fact that we are much greater than what we see, hear or reason ourselves to be. The sum of what we are cannot be considered or believed when we look at what the body suggests to us we are. He tells us that we are more than anything we can ever reason ourselves to be. We are greater, more powerful, more God-like, more perfected than our reasoning can encompass. How vast is their sum! And he didn't come to that realization by way of reasoning.

And in verse 18 David comes to realize that the thoughts God has of us are not limited to just the ones He had yesterday or last week or last month. He says they like are more in number than the sand.

"Oh, Lord, Our Lord, how majestic is your name in all the earth. When I consider your heavens, the work of your fingers, the moon and the stars, which you have ordained, What is man that thou art mindful of him?

Man is my creation in whom I have placed the seasoning of heaven to be spread throughout the earth. He has been endued with power and purpose and potential. I live in him. (Know ye not that your body is the temple of the Holy Spirit who lives IN you?) I am man's seasoning. I am that which is superior to his reasoning. I am his wisdom and understanding and strength and keeper. I am his creator and the supernatural engineer who created and assembled him just for my own purpose.

Man is divinely seasoned to do a work that nothing else in creation can do. He is My ambassador and My child. He is My assigned and uniquely equipped vessel to stand in My stead in the earth realm. When he stands in My stead, I stand in him and he and I become one. Thus, I am in him and he is in me through his faith in My word.

I am He who seasons him to excel beyond his own reasoning. I am He who has decreed that nothing shall be impossible unto My believer, no matter how unreasonable it appears.

You are God's seasoning to the world. Come let us reason together that our reasoning will cause you to know, recognize and walk in God's divine seasoning upon your life. Don't let your reasoning spoil your seasoning. Blessings.

The Lord our God is a man of War.
He is strong and mighty in battle.
He teaches my hands to war.

Ready! Aim! FIRE!

I read a post by someone tonight which encouraged its readers to take no spiritual prisoners from the kingdom of darkness, but to use the bullets in our spiritual funs to perform a live fire against the enemy every chance you get.

How true this concept is. I can remember my old Army days when the division training officer would perform mock engagement encounters with a fabricated enemy. Basically what you did was to engage the enemy by way of "paper" or in theory, but not by way of face to face, win or lose, confrontation. This was usually done in order to prepare for actual engagements and/or to preserve or re-allocate fiscal funds to more important matters. However, it doesn't matter how many "mock" battles you fight and how much theory you know, until you actually hit the battlefield and oppose your enemy face-to-face you have no actual personal proof that what you believe is better and superior to the ways, methods, strategies and devices of your adversary. Theory only teaches us how things "ought to" work, while practical application actually proves to us that what we believe or practice or theorize actually does work when properly applied.

That is where we now stand with the devil and the battle we are all a part of. As believers we have theory. The Bible is our theory. Don't misunderstand me. I'm not saying the Bible IS theory. I'm saying the Bible is our theory until we decide to apply it to every situation in our life. For even the Word of God tells us that this same gospel that was preached to you was also preached to them (non-believers), but it produced no fruit in them because having heard it they did not mix it with faith (works done predicated on beliefs in the principles and laws of God).

The Word of God, unless applied to our lives is nothing more than good information not received or acted upon. The application of the Word of God runs a very simple course in our lives. When we apply it, the application of the information will bring about revelation which will produce manifestation and yield in each of us a higher level of spiritual consecration. But until the application takes place we will remain in a state of spiritual sterilization (void of powerful spiritual experiences).

This is why we can no longer voluntarily and happily remain in the theory phase of the Word of God. We, as believers, must take the weapon of our righteousness and load it with the Word of God and put the devil in the crosshairs of our spiritual scopes and pull the trigger of faith sending our Word projectile down range and directly into the wicked and deceitful heart of our adversary. We've got to unload on him just the way he tries to unload sin and destruction and doubt and havoc and sickness unto us every day.

We are not just ambassadors for Christ but we are also mercenaries of the cross. It is our job to enter into battle on behalf of righteousness and to take no spiritual (demonic) prisoners. We cannot permit ourselves to become complacent and comfortable in the false security of the foxhole of do nothingness. As Dr. Martin Luther King, Jr. once said, ". . . we cannot allow ourselves to become bogged down in the paralysis of analysis." If it doesn't line up with the Word of God, as a marksman for Christ, shoot it. If it represents a doctrine other than the one Christ taught, shoot it. If it does not declare Christ as our Lord and Savior and God as the Creator of all, unload on it. You cannot play around with this enemy. He's cunning. He's deceptive. He's persistent. He's dangerous. And he's mad at you.

His sights are set on you. His purpose is to destroy you. His presence is to steal, kill and destroy all that has been given unto you. His plan is to deceive you. His motive is to deny and destroy your blissful eternity. His goal is to take you out and then to go after all of your love ones one by one. There is no love between you and him. There is no friendship between you and him. There is no honor between you and him. He is constantly trying to set his crosshairs on your heart. He's aiming at your children. He's eyeing your marriage. He's focusing on your future. He's plotting attacks against your health. He's seeking your happiness. He's strategizing against your salvation.

What a mistake it would be for you to get him in the crosshairs of your prayers, in the crosshairs of your authority, in the crosshairs of your divine powers and then to lower your spiritual weapon of faith and let the most sought after enemy in the history of creation escape. Believers, you've got to come from behind the desks and out of the offices and go onto the streets and onto the battlefields and test your weapon of faith, and your weapon of joy and your weapon of peace and your weapon of prayer and your weapon of consecration and your weapon of knowledge and application of the Word of God.

It is the Word of God, your only effective weapon against this enemy, which will render you the victor in this campaign. We must be like the Marines who raised the flag at Iwo Jima during the middle of one of the bloodiest battles of the war. We must raise the banner of righteousness and let the devil know that it is by our application and not our theory that we TAKE this territory by force for the Kingdom of Light and that we will never submit, surrender or retreat from it one step because we came to pursuit, to overtake and to reign supreme as warriors for the Kingdom of Light. As the words of the old hymn reminds us:

```
Onward, Christian soldiers, marching as to war,
with the cross of Jesus going on before.
Christ, the royal Master, leads against the foe;
forward into battle see his banners go!
```

A Better You and A Better Christian

Refrain:

Onward, Christian soldiers, marching as to war, with the cross of Jesus going on before.

At the sign of triumph Satan's host doth flee; on then, Christian soldiers, on to victory!
Hell's foundations quiver at the shout of praise; brothers, lift your voices, loud your anthems raise.

Like a mighty army moves the church of God; brothers, we are treading where the saints have trod.
We are not divided, all one body we, one in hope and doctrine, one in charity.

Crowns and thrones may perish, kingdoms rise and wane, but the church of Jesus constant will remain. Gates of hell can never gainst that church prevail; we have Christ's own promise, and that cannot fail.

Onward then, ye people, join our happy throng, blend with ours your voices in the triumph song. Glory, laud, and honor unto Christ the King, this through countless ages men and angels sing.

Let us continue to always fight the good fight of faith!

Blessings.

But though we, or an angel from heaven, preach any other gospel (doctrine) unto you than that which we have preached unto you, let him be accursed.

There Is Only One True Doctrine

DOCTRINE: Christian truth and teaching passed on from generation to generation as "the faith (doctrine) that was delivered to the saints" (Jude 3).

Believers, I have a simple question this morning, and that is in what doctrine are you placing your deepest faith and confidence? Upon what doctrine do you trust and rely in every aspect of your life? Doctrine is the single most important thing that you have as a believer. It is doctrine which teaches us about our redemption. Doctrine teaches us about our rescue from sin. Doctrine teaches us about salvation. Doctrine teaches us about heavenly tongues and divine power. Doctrine teaches us about who we are in Christ. Doctrine teaches us about salvation. Doctrine is the system upon which all of our beliefs and convictions rest. Doctrine!! Doctrine instructs us in faithfulness. Doctrine mandates our steadfastness. Doctrine!!

Doctrine is neither ". . . academic or practical, outdated or contemporary, conventional or ruthless, argumentative or suggestive." Rather, doctrine is simply God ordained truth. And this truth, just as it was left to us by Christ, that is without any diluting, altering or compromising elements, is deemed so important to the kingdom of God that His inspired scripture teaches us that "If there comes any unto you, and brings not this doctrine, receive him not into your house, neither bid him God's speed for he that biddeth him God's speed is a partaker in his evil deed." (Evil deed= spreading of another doctrine.) The Word of Truth goes on to teach us that "But though we, or an angel from heaven, preach any other gospel (doctrine) unto you than that which we have preached unto you, let him be accursed."

Sure people will look at you like you're crazy when you evangelize, teach, preach or even pass on the doctrine of Christ in casual conversation, but that is still our responsibility as believers. Did not they do the same to Christ? Examine what Mark 1:21 says: "And they were astonished at his doctrine: for he taught them as one that had authority, and not as the scribes." Notice ". . . and not as the scribes". Why not as the Scribes? Because the Scribes taught as ones who were possessed with knowledge and schooling and philosophies and man-engineered laws and doctrines. But Christ, knowing the power and authority which were inherent in the Gospel of God spoke a doctrine that empowered all who believed upon it to do just as He did and accomplish just what He accomplished. This is why Jesus questioned Nicodemus as such: "Nicodemus, art thou a teacher of the Jews and know ye not these things?" In other words, Nicodemus, you're the one who is suppose to be teaching these things and this doctrine to others, and yet you do not know them yourself. (Therefore, what doctrine were the Jews teaching then?)

In the book of Mark (1:27) you will notice that people were so accustomed to adhering to some manmade doctrine they actually referred to the doctrine of Christ as a "new doctrine." Was Christ's DOCTRINE new? No it was not. This doctrine was actually released in the earth realm and over mankind when God, in the book of Genesis, gave man dominion (total legal authority and power) over all of the creation. The doctrine that Christ brought to us is the same doctrine that God gave to and left with us in Eden. It has never changed. It still works the very same way, but it will not work for you if you do not believe in it, receive it and operate (by faith) in it.

Review Jesus's words (John 7:17-18) and see for yourself: Jesus answered them, and said, *My DOCTRINE is not mine, but his that sent me. If any man will do his will, he shall know of the DOCTRINE, whether it be of God, or whether I speak of myself.* (Do his will=obey the teachings of the doctrine.)

Why were the apostles able to manifest the great and numerous miracles that they were and as you and I should also be? There are two scriptures that will help us to accurately answer this question. First there is Matthew 28:18-20: Go ye therefore and teach all nations, baptizing them in the name of the Father, and of the Son, and of the Holy Ghost: <u>Teaching them to observe all things WHATSOEVER I have commanded you</u>.

It is the latter part of this that is so pertinent to our discussion here. Jesus told his disciples to TEACH people (how to) observe (or to diligently put into practice) everything that he had commanded or taught them. Now what had he commanded or taught them? The doctrine of the Kingdom of God, which when received and practiced, automatically empowers, illuminates and transforms.

The second reason can be found in Acts 2:42: "And they continued stedfastly in the Apostles doctrine and fellowship, and in breaking of bread and in prayer." That is to say, they continued unmoved in the doctrine left by Christ with his apostles. They met (assembling with other believers), broke bread (ate together) and prayed together. They gave no place or chance for another doctrine to enter among them.

How important is doctrine to God AND to you? Romans 16:17-18 says: I beseech you, brethren, mark them which cause divisions and offences contrary to the doctrine which ye have learned and avoid them for they that are such serve not our Lord Jesus Christ . . . and (go about with their) eloquent speech deceiving the hearts of the simple (spiritually unlearned).

Doctrine is too important for believers to not know it. It doesn't matter what organization you wish to join, you must be indoctrinated into it. And if you refuse to accept and abide by the organization's doctrine, you will never be regarded as a fully faithful and committed member. It is no different in the Kingdom of God. God's doctrine are his rules, His laws, His requirements, His expectations, His empowerment, His virtue. It is what makes us like him. We accept his every rule, law, guideline, statue and principle. And then we obey them. Thus, via our obedience his kingdom come on earth just as it is in heaven. And it did so through you because you are a doctrine walking, doctrine talking, doctrine living, doctrine praying, doctrine manifesting, doctrine believing child of the most high.

What's your doctrine? Do you really have one? Is it the doctrine that Christ left for us? If not, then you have no real, sure, proven, eternal doctrine. I leave you with the wisdom of these three verses: For the time will come when they will not endure sound doctrine, but after their own lusts shall they heap to themselves teachers, having itching ears.

Whosoever transgresseth and abideth not in the doctrine of Christ, hath not God. He that abideth in the doctrine of Christ, he hath both the Father and the Son. And this Gospel (doctrine) of the kingdom shall be preached in all the world for a witness unto all nations, and then shall the end (of time) come.

Blessings.

David was greatly distressed because the men were talking of stoning him; each one was bitter in spirit because of his sons and daughters. But David found strength in the LORD his God.

ENCOURAGING YOURSELF
IN THE LORD

I am reminded of a passage of scripture, (1 Sam 30:1-8) wherein David, a man after God's own heart, returning to his own city, discovered that in the absence of the men of his city, his enemies attacked and carried away into captivity all of the ladies and children. Instantly, many who knew and had served with David became depressed and began to despair at what had happened in their absence. David's men became so depressed and despaired so badly that they began to assign fault and blame for what had occurred. Many of them raised their voices as well as their hands against David and wished to stone him because he was their leader and they held him accountable and responsible for what had happened though he neither had the power to stop it nor was any more pleased by it than they were.

The men wept. The strong fighting men cried. Warriors were weakened and reduced to strengthless men of tears and sobs. Many of them yelled, "Kill David! Kill David! Away with him! Stone him! Stone him! Death to our leader who has caused this tragedy to befall us!" And nowhere in that passage of scripture does the Bible give us any insight into one person in whom David could confide. Nowhere does it say there was one in whom David could find consolation. Of all the strong men who had been with David and even been in battle with him, not a single one is recorded in the word of God as emerging as a support system for David during one of the most trying times of his entire life. Conversely, the Bible even reveals to us that even David himself was highly distressed at what had occurred because he himself had two wives who'd been taken by the camp's invaders. He did not know what to do. He had no one to whom to turn. There was no confidant to be found among all of his men. He was hurt. He was grieving. He was without support. He had lost not one but TWO wives. His people had turned on him in an instant. His very life was in danger of being taken by his own angry men.

But thanks be to God, God's word, in a simple seldom recognized or quoted sentence, shows us how David managed to get through his toughest battle. The answer can be found in 1 Samuel 30:6 where the Bible teaches us that ". . . but David encouraged himself in the Lord his God." Yes! That is the answer! With no prayer warriors to meet and pray with, with no elder to lay hands on him, with no chaplain to counsel with him, with no choir or praise and worship team to sing him happy, with no teacher to expound upon the word, with no prophet to speak into his life and yet while undergoing the worst of possible conditions and even having to fight for his own life, David, ENCOURAGED HIMSELF in the Lord his God. He did not allow the situation to alter his relationship with or his faith in the Lord his God. When everyone else doubted and even wanted to kill him, he yet encouraged himself in the Lord. When all around him appeared to be a disaster and at a loss for sure, he yet encouraged himself.

Not only did he encourage himself, but at such a time as this, he even YET asked for further instructions and directions from God. An examination of the next two verses will show us that David never wavered in his faith. He asked that the ephod be brought to him and he prepared himself for prayer and meditation. And in the prayer he asked a very important question. He says, "Shall I pursue after this troop?" Notice, he never asked, if he could have a break or time to mourn or just a little while to get himself together. Rather, in spite of everything that is going on his life, he immediately turned and asked the Father, what would you have me to do next?

The beauty of this question can only be realized when you read God's immediate response to David's inquiry. God says, pursue and surely you shall overtake them. Pursue. When? Now? Even while folks are doubting you—pursue. Even while it's looking doubtful and maybe even downright unwinnable—pursue. While tears are running down your chin—pursue. While you are in pain—pursue. While your home is experiencing turmoil, health seems to be failing, friends seem to be abandoning, family is distancing themselves and fellow Christians seem to be calling for your stoning too—pursue. Why? Because if you get up out of yourself pity, and out of your abode of distress and out of your habitat of doubt, God himself will empower you to OVERTAKE, defeat and reign victorious over that which seems to have a victory over you right now.

As Christians, we don't have time to sit and pout and ponder. We have to pursue. We can't spend time and energy focusing on the events of the past. Both our time and energy must be highly focused in on the battles that are presently before us. We all wish to have someone there to speak encouraging words into our lives. However, that might not always be the case for all of us. We all wish to be able to pick and choose our battles. But, again, that might not be the case for most of us either. We fight what we must because we must fight the fights that are before us.

Men and women of the most high God I charge you to gird your loins and put on the whole amour of God that having done all to stand you will be able to stand and stand and stand through the power, might, wisdom and guidance of Christ Jesus who gives us His power that we as His representatives might be able to do all good things. Trust him. Believe him. Serve him with your whole mind, heart, spirit and all of your natural and spiritual strengths. Let nothing separate you from the Love of Jesus our Christ. And remain confident that He who will never leave nor forsake you has made you to be more than a conqueror in all of these things (battles). Speak faith-filled words and believe and receive every promise of God our Father. Encourage yourself in the Lord that you may be found worthy and able to encourage others during their times of need and/or distress. Blessings in the unmatchable name of Jesus the only Christ that was, is or shall ever be.

Blessings.

YES! "I CAN DO <u>ALL</u> THINGS THROUGH CHRIST JESUS WHO STRENGTHENS ME."

Beware of the tiny foxes lest they destroy
the vineyard of your spirit

Blessed are the pure in heart, for they will see God

FOREIGN OBJECT DAMAGE

I cannot begin this teaching without first harkening back to an event which will serve as the cornerstone example for this word. The example to which I am referring is the one in which American Airline pilot Captain Chesley Sullenburger, the pilot in command of American Airline flight #1549, was forced, in order to save the lives of hundreds of AA passengers aboard the aircraft which he was piloting, to perform a ditching (controlled unauthorized landing away from a runway) of his aircraft due to a bird strike.

Now a reasonable person would naturally and immediately pose the very logical question, why did an entire plane have to be ditched in a river just because a small and insignificant bird became entangled in one of its massive multi-million dollar engines? Could not the plane have proceeded on to its destiny and performed its mission in accordance with its flight plane? And how were all of those who were on board endangered by a simply bird strike? And most importantly, what does this have to do with my salvation, purpose and obedience to God? Can there be a connection between a bird strike and my walk with Christ. Let's see.

First, let's establish that Capt. Sully, as he is commonly called, is a highly capable, extremely knowledgeable, and exceptionally qualified instruments qualified pilot. He has many years of flight experience and has logged a massive number of flight hours in both the pilot in command and the co-pilot seats. He is seasoned and qualified for this flight. He has spent a number of hours in the flight simulator, pilot training, and flying re-fresher and check flights. He is no stranger or novice to what he is doing. Yet, a small and insignificant bird causes him to have to either ditch his aircraft or crash and burn with numerous other lives at stakes as well.

The plane that he flew had to be ditched because the engine ingested something that it was not specifically designed to intake; this ingestion caused the engine to loose it overall power or effectiveness. It lost its ability to produce the power need to provide the lift and thrust to the aircraft. It lost its ability to continue to take in, compress and expel ambient air which is what it was designed to do and is what the plane needs it to do if propulsion is to provided to it. The most significant idea to remember here is that if an engine stops producing operating mechanical power to the aircraft, it is no longer any good to the aircraft.

Ironically, huge, powerful, multi-million dollar engines can be very easily incapacitated if any object other than those that were specifically designed to work with the engine are taken in by the engine. These objects are commonly referred to as "foreign objects" because they are foreign to the construction and maximum operation of an aircraft engine. The smallest of these objects are extremely dangerous to an aircraft image and can with very little effort completely render one of these powerful mechanical devices inoperable or even destroyed. The official cause in pilots' language would read something like this: destruction of asset due to foreign object damage. (You see foreign object damage is nothing more than when an aircraft's engine ingests or sucks in or takes in by any mean, an object that should not be there. A formal or book definition defines F.O.D. as "Damage that is caused by a substance, debris, or an article which is alien to an engine or system which causes it to function in a decreased, weakened, less effective or perhaps even a totally inoperable fashion."

Likewise, you have been perfectly crafted by God. You are His handiwork, created and ordained before the foundation of the world unto good works. Like Capt. Sulley are capable, knowledgeable and highly capable. But for some reason (many believers say from time to time), it just doesn't seem as if I'm there yet. It doesn't seem as if I'm doing what I know I'm suppose to be doing for the Kingdom. Sometimes I even feel as if I'm letting God down. I know I can do more, but for some reason, I'm not.

I submit to you this is true usually because of F.O.D in our spiritual lives. Our F.O.D. is not like the aircraft's F.O.D. The pilot could easily spot the flock of birds through which he flew or a piece of debris that was ingested while taxing on the runway on the way to takeoff. But since we wrestle not against flesh and blood, how, then, can we see and identify our spiritual F.O.D. How do we know when we've taken in the wrong thing or ingest something that will derail our walk with Christ? And who is responsible in the spirit realm for ensuring that there is no spiritual F.O.D. in my life?

Remembering, of course, that spiritual foreign objects are not always easily recognizable. Sometimes they are hidden in our traditions. Sometimes we allow them to find a secluded place out of our vision because we have allowed our spiritual eyes to become dimmed. Sometimes we even permit them a passage into our lives because we stop praying, praising and worshipping. Our faith becomes diminished, our hope begins to wane and our Godly confidence diminishes. And with each of these there comes a corresponding Foreign Object. The foreign objects that your praise use to destroy or at least keep at bay (since you're no praising any more) have little to no resistance finding their way into your spiritual life. The foreign objects that your exalting and worship use to bind and keep out of your life, now are an everyday part of your life. Your once fervent prayers are not longer seasoned with the power and fervency that they once possessed. Your testimonies are now few and far between and your studying of God word is more of a task than a treasure. Why? Because F.O.D. has entered into your spirit and is now causing you to operate a level that is far below that which you were created and ordained to carry out. In other words a spiritual substance, debris or article, which is alien to you and your purpose as a child of God, has entered into your life and is now causing you to function in a decreased, weakened, less effective or perhaps even a totally inoperable fashion.

Let's get this straight. Whether you agree or disagree with the analogy provided in this teaching, know for certain that spiritual F.O.D. is real and is a trick of the adversary. Spiritual F.O.D. will indeed destroy your walk with Christ.

The Word of God Himself, teaches us to "Keep they heart with all diligence." (Proverbs 4:23) Why does the Word teach us to keep or guard our hearts with all diligence? Because it is the heart of man which houses the sincerity and the essence of a person. That is why God has taught us that we look upon the outside of a person and attempt to judge him/her based upon what the external shows. But He goes on to tell us that He looks on the inside (at the heart of man) and He judges man based upon his heart and not his appearance. But how many of us has judged somebody because they didn't "look saved" or "dressed like a Christian" or whatever. F.O.D.

Why does God tell us to "keep or guard" our heart. Because He doesn't want us to protect or to exercise sound stewardship over our heart one day and then relent on our standards the next. It is essential that we KEEP our heart with all diligence (hard work, patience and purposefulness) understanding that it is "A man's heart [which] deviseth his way." (Proverbs 16:9) Wrong heart—wrong way. Right heart—right way." This simply means that whatever you allow to enter your heart will ultimately lead and guide you and control your behavior, thoughts, speech and destiny.

Years ago we use to say, "Garbage in, garbage out." When it comes to the spirit that still holds true. If you continue to forsake to guard your heart with all diligence, you will invariably, sooner or later, allow something that is counter to Holiness to enter into it. And when it does, you will know because it will instantly manifest itself in your thoughts, deeds and speech. "For out of the abundance of the heart the mouth doth speak" (Luke 6:45).

Believers should also know that it does not take very much leaven (F.O.D.) to destroy your spiritual walk as Galatians 5:9 teaches us that "A little leaven leavens the whole lump," and Song of Solomon 2:15 reminds us that it is "*The small foxes* (little bits of F.O.D.) *destroy the vines* (our connection to Christ).

Unforgiveness is an F.O.D. Pride is an F.O.D. Doubt is an F.O.D. Fear is an F.O.D. Love of the world and its offerings is an F.O.D. A lack of spiritual integrity is an F.O.D. Weak prayer life is an F.O.D. Disobedience to the Word of God is an F.O.D. Not assembling with other believers is an F.O.D. Not studying the word of God is an F.O.D. Being religious rather than relational is an F.O.D. Unfaithfulness is an F.O.D. Rebelliousness is an F.O.D. Leaning to your own understanding is an F.O.D. Trusting the mind over the spirit is an F.O.D. Not receiving every Word of Christ and what He has already accomplished for you as a result of His birth, ministry, suffering death, resurrection and ascension as spiritual truth is an F.O.D. Unbelief in the statues of God is an F.O.D. Not spending time with God daily is an F.O.D. And so are refusing to praise and worship, making and accepting excuses rather than exercising and developing your faith in God, not knowing who you are and whose you are, not guarding your heart diligently and not being fully persuaded that this is exactly and only what you want to do with your life (be a Christian and disciple) here on earth. All of these are sure signs that you're suffering from F.O.D. and if you don't soon ditch yourself at the alter, you will certainly crash and burn and, quite possibly, take others down with you.

And it is extremely easy for these (and other) spiritual F.O.D.'s to enter into our spiritual lives if we are not aware that these are simply wiles of the devil. This is why we must diligently guard the gates to our heart (our mind, eyes, ears, mouth, and even emotions). But according to John fifteenth chapter, if we remain connected to the source, we will be able to do much. Once we become disconnect that is when the objects have their legal access into our lives.

Believers, don't allow bad, inaccurate or traditional teachings to cause you to lower your guard and permit the entrance of F.O.D. into your spiritual walk! Rebuke it! For 1 Corinthians 9:27 warns us that is very possible to teach this doctrine and gospel and come the day of judgment find myself a castaway. Please do not allow F.O.D. to claim this victory over your life.

A flight plan has been filed for your aircraft (earthly body). You are the pilot in command. All of your instruments are fully functional—your spirit, God's grace, His guidance and His path (will for your life) are all at work on your behalf. Trust them and lean not to your own understanding, but acknowledge Him in all of your ways and doings and He will certainly land you safely at your destination and free of all F.O.D.

> Yield not to temptation for yielding is sin,
> each victory will help you some other to win.
> Fight manwardly onward, dull passions subdue,
> look ever to Jesus (not your mind, not your ability, not your
> traditions, not your own understanding) but look ever to
> JESUS AND JESUS will see you through. Blessings.

And God said, "Let us create man in our
image and in our likeness"

Therefore, *if any man be in Christ*, he is a new creature: old
things are passed away; behold, all things are become new!

I've Got a New Pair of Genes

I remember walking down the road as a little boy hand in hand with my daddy as we headed for the barber shop to get our (then) 65 cents haircuts when suddenly our neighbor called out to him, "Mr. Williams, even if I didn't already know that was your boy, all I would have to do would be to look at him just one time and I'd know from then on that you were his daddy, because youall are exactly alike. He is the splitting image you and no doubt you have passed on all of your best on to him." The significance of this statement didn't hit me until many, many decades later after I'd become saved and accepted God as my Father.

When people saw me, they saw my daddy. When I spoke, I sounded like my daddy. My behavior was modeled and shaped by and after my daddy's. My thinking was along the lines of my daddy's. My interactions were like my daddy's. And as a result, I appeared to people to be just like my daddy.

Now that I am saved and have the right to call God my Father, why should this change? Why should I not look like God in the flesh? Why should I not think and behave like the child of the Most High Father? Why should I not act and re-act to all things as does my Father? I really believe that is the case with many believers because we have forgotten that just as in the natural, we have a spiritual genetic makeup that we have received from our

Father which passes on the traits of the parents (our Father who art in heaven) to the child. Thus is the nature and responsibility of genetics.

It is funny how we recognize that we inherited certain natural genetic traits and pre-dispositions from our natural parents, but we disregard this as being possible in the spirit realm. We know that we are of our ethnicity because of the ethnicity of our parents, but we disregard this when it comes to the ethnicity (spirit being) of our Father. We understand that we inherited certain attributes, traits and abilities directly from our natural parents, but we disregard the very same idea when it comes to inheriting spiritual powers, authority and abilities from God our Father. How can this be?

We accept the fact that we are black, dark, light, skinny, fat, athletic, scholarly or whatever else because of the propensities of our parents along those lines. Yet we refute that we are mighty, miracle workers, healers, rulers, princes and princesses, filled with wisdom and knowledgeable above imagination as a result of what your Father has passed on to you in the form of your spiritual genes.

Anyone who believes in God is not "average" because they now have a new pair of (spiritual) genes out of which they are able to operate and to bring about things and events that "average" people cannot. Is it any wonder that Jesus said that nothing shall be impossible to those who believe? Is it any wonder that He told us to call those things that be not as though they were. Is it any wonder that He told us that these signs shall follow those who believe: In my name shall they cast out devils; they shall speak with new tongues and if they drink any deadly thing, it shall not hurt them; they shall lay hands on the sick, and they shall recover?

How, then, are you able to do these things? By your natural abilities? No. By your own design? No. By your own institutional theological training? No. You are able to do it by the power of the Holy Ghost which dwells within you because you are now a child (meaning a seed or offspring) of God Himself and, thus, have been empowered by way of your Holy Father's genes and power to do great and awesome works.

No one is surprised when a famous athlete's son follows in the footsteps of his father and becomes a super athlete as well. Neither is anyone shocked when a famous actor's or actress's child gets a leading role in a movie. No one utters a single word when a successful businessman's offspring continues his father's business ventures. Why, then, does it seem so far-fetched when children of God carry on their Father's business? ("Know ye not that I must be about my Father's business.) Miracles is your business. Healing is your business. Fervent prayer is your business. Ministry is your business. Letting your light so shine that men may see your good works and worship your Father in heaven is your business. Praying the sick back to good and wholesome health is your business. Speaking in new tongues is your business. And if you are a true child of the Most High, then you are spiritually genetically predisposed to do these things. It happened the day you received Christ as your savior and God as your Father. The problem is that you are a new creature, but you are still operating out of old genes; that is to say, you're carrying new wine in your old bottle.

My sisters and brothers, when God blew his Spirit into Adam (A'dom which actually means mankind), he wasn't just blowing oxygen. God actually blew a portion of Himself into our earthen vessel (which is why we have this treasure in these earthen vessels). Literally He made Adam a carbon copy of Himself and then told Adam and Eve (Eve means giver of life; thus the names Adam and Eve together literally mean the givers of life to all of mankind) to reproduce and to subdue all things and to have absolute power and authority (dominion) over them. God literally personally and directly empowered man to do and to be so when He blew a portion of Himself (His genetic and divinely majestic self) into the physical makeup of man.

Did not God tell us that the life of the flesh is in the blood? What is in the blood? The breath of life. Our God-likeness is within us. It is there to empower every cell and sub-atomic element of our being, both natural and physical. (He has given unto us all things pertaining unto life and Godliness.) And if any portion of our body is denied access to what is in the blood, it begins to die immediately. Even our great and wonderful brain can operate only a short timeframe without the oxygen (breath of life) God gave to all mankind through direct interaction with Adam and continues it today to the off-springs of every one of the first couple's distant children.

Your are uniquely and wonderfully made. Science will never be able to teach you the true realities the depth, width or height of your makeup. Philosophy and technology are not capable of revealing it to you. Theology schools can't touch it, and men of God seem to be afraid to teach it. Unless you know whose you are, you will never know who you are. If you don't know your daddy, then it will do you no good for people to say you look like Him, because you don't know the one whom you resemble or whose gene pool you possess.

If you are a believer, you have the best of the best in your spiritual gene pool. Why are walking around wasting your Father's genetic transference? Believe in our yourself, in your Father, in Your genetic inheritance and in your spiritually genetic capabilities and duties. And remember, when you accepted God as your Father, he adopted You and gave you His genes as part of your inheritance. Now arrest your fear and doubt and walk in the power of your new genes—in Jesus name!

Blessings.

I surrender all. I surrender all. All to Jesus, my blessed Savior, I surrender ALL.

GIVING UP TO GOD

What does it really mean to surrender to You, God?

What does it really mean to willingly come under the total power, dominion, authority and guidance of someone other than myself?

If I surrender to You, can I still think my own thoughts?

If I surrender to You, can I still chart my own path?

If I surrender to You, can I still be controlled by own emotions? History? Traditions?

Can I still manage my own time as I please? Or do I now have any time that is truly mine?

Can I worship as it suits me or must I now follow the dictates of Him to whom I have surrendered?

Whose laws am I subject to if I surrender?

Whose statues must I keep?

Whose word must I obey?

If I am surrender, can I continue to hate? To lie? To steal? To gossip? To live contrary to Your commands?

If I surrender to you, can my heart still fight against Your ways?

And must my ears listen only to hear the voice of You, my real and only Master?

When I am surrendered, will not pray leap from my lips daily? And will not faith abound in all that I say and do?

Because I have surrendered I have no will of my own except to remain in the true will of my captor.

But because I have surrendered, You now fight for me, and care for me, and provide me with all things that I need. For thus is the role of the captor toward his surrendered captive.

You are my captor and thus my provider, my peace, my provisions, my protection, my mouthpiece, my hope and my guide.

I surrender all that I have to You, God. You are my greatest captor ever. Help me to remain surrendered to You at all times and at all costs. For to leave the assurance of Your captivity is to leave the only true beacon of hope, love, protection and absolute power ever. Thank you, God for choosing me to be your captive prisoner of righteousness.

> All to Jesus I surrender;
> All to Him I freely give;
> I will ever love and trust Him,
> In His presence daily live.

(Refrain)
I surrender all,
I surrender all;
All to Thee, my blessed Savior,
I surrender all.

All to Jesus I surrender;
Humbly at His feet I bow,
Worldly pleasures all forsaken;
Take me, Jesus, take me now.

All to Jesus I surrender;
Make me, Savior, wholly Thine;
Let me feel the Holy Spirit,
Truly know that Thou art mine.

All to Jesus I surrender;
Lord, I give myself to Thee;
Fill me with Thy love and power;
Let Thy blessing fall on me.

All to Jesus I surrender;
Now I feel the sacred flame.
Oh, the joy of full salvation!
Glory, glory, to His Name!

(Refrain)
I surrender all,
I surrender all;
All to Thee, my blessed Savior,
I surrender all.

Samuel Williams

He Still Loves Me!

YES JESUS LOVES ME

Jesus loves me
This I know,
For the Bible tells me so.
Little ones to Him belong;
They are weak but He is strong.

Jesus loves me!
Loves me still,
Tho I'm very weak and ill,
That I might from sin be free,
Bled and died upon the tree.

Jesus loves me!
He who died
Heaven's gate to open wide;
He will wash away my sin,
Let His little child come in.

Jesus loves me!
He will stay
Close beside me all the way.
Thou hast bled and died for me;
I will henceforth live for Thee.

Chorus:
Yes, Jesus loves me!
Yes, Jesus loves me!
Yes, Jesus loves me!
The Bible tells me so.

—Anna B. Warner, 1820-1915

(Written by A.B. Warner to comfort the heart of a dying child. Set to music one year later by a composer and released as a selection in a hymnal.)

GOD, WE THANK YOU!

God, with all that is within us, we thank You.

We thank You for every reason and season You have purposed in our lives.

We thank You for every creation You have ordained to be.

We thank You for the sky, the wind, the firmaments, and every sea.

We thank You for sharing Your spirit, image and likeness with humankind.

We thank You for sharing Your endless mercy and agape love with us.

We thank You for Your timeless immutability in which we can confidently trust.

We thank You for your compassion and grace and Your wisdom and salvation.

We thank You for the words, works, and hope left us by Jesus Your son.

We thank You for redemption and forgiveness in-spite of the wrongs we've done.

We thank You for sharing your Holy Spirit and Your divine will.

We thank You for sharing your yolk breaking anointing and power.

We thank You for your constant counsel every minute of every hour.

We thank You for all you are which is more than we can say.

We thank You for protection day after day.

We thank You for your purpose and your might.

We thank You, God, for keeping us all day and all night.

With all that is within us, we thank You.

For Your caressing touch and gentle midnight talks.

For giving us a desire to follow You and to remain Your salt.

Blessings.

The Well Need Not a Physician

God, who else could do for me what you do?

Who else could take the old me and make it new?

What physician could have rid me of my supernatural diseases

And yet take no pay because it sincerely pleases

His heart, his will, his purpose and his cause to see me whole?

You did, God. You did. And I thank You for being the physician of my soul.

COMPLETE ACCOUNTABILITY

Accountability: The act of personally accepting full responsibility for every spoken word or deed performed while in our suit of flesh.

"So then each one of us shall give account of himself to God."

COMPLETE ACCOUNTABILITY

Originally I started this writing off by quoting several different scriptures. But, while reflecting upon what I'd written, the Holy Spirit spoke to me and said, "Just as Jesus asked His disciples 'Whom do men say that I am?' and just as He asked them 'Whom do you say I am?' I now ask you, My child, from the depth of your spirit and with all that is within you, tell me this thing that I now ask you, and that is what is accountability and to whom and for what are you held accountable? This," the Spirit said, "is the critical knowledge my people are failing to remember and earnestly embrace."

Natural versus Spiritual Accountability

In the natural sense, accountability simply means giving a report of details on the condition, locations, and status of your or another's assets. In the natural, it means being able to be held personally responsible and professionally liable for something of value that has been entrusted into your care for safeguarding, stewardship over, management and protection of or perhaps even the nurturing and development of. Ultimately, in the natural, the term accountability refers to one's ability to be held solely and overall liable and responsible for the condition, treatment, and preservation, or overall quality or condition of an entrusted commodity.

Yet, though, in the spiritual sense the term accountability takes on a vastly different meaning as well as role. From a spiritual perspective accountability indicates the degree to which we have exercised our love, faith, loyalty, commitment, and obedience to God as indicated by every work each believer has done while serving in the flesh.

In order to understand accountability, we must first come to understand that our works can never exceed our TRUE FAITH level. Consequently, our TRUE FAITH level directly serves as the cap or peak of our ability to obey what God commands of us. How significant is this to a believer and his accountability? Consider Jesus' words: "If you love me, then keep my commandments." In every day terminology Jesus was simply challenging us as thus: If you truly love me, then prove it to me by keeping my commandments.

God! If that is the case, how, then can we love You if our faith is not sufficient to permit us to keep Your commandments? And if we can't keep your commandments, how, then, can we ever summon the requisite degree of faith to "ACT" (actually command and receive the results that you desire of us) like someone created in your image and likeness? And if we cannot do this, how, then, can we ever represent to the dying world the empowering anointing of the Holy Ghost in our lives if our TRUE FAITH level is insufficient to allow us to live a life (let our light so shine that men will see it and ask "What must I do to be saved?") that reflects the God and His ability in us? Yet, though, despite our shortfalls, we are still 100% accountable to God for all that we have done or failed to do while serving as His ambassadors in this suit of flesh.

Now what does it mean to be accountable to God? In Revelations (the book whose name means a revealed or shared truth), John wrote, "And I saw standing before the throne the great and small, and each one gave account for his deeds while he was in the flesh." In other words, God shared with John a truth which revealed that every man, woman, boy, and girl, ultimately will have to stand before God Himself and give an account for his or her every deed, thought, and action in order to determine his or her eternal destination.

Why And To Whom Must We Account?

But why? Why would God judge believers so sternly on the basis of a single report or account? Why is what I've done in the flesh so important to God that by it, He would determine my heavenly reward. Again consider the scriptures which reminds us of the following Biblical facts:

1. This earth is not our home. We are but strangers passing through.
2. We are ambassadors for God's kingdom who were chosen and called unto God's works before the formation of the earth.
3. We were ordained, predestined, and thoroughly equipped to do the work of God in the earth realm before the rebellion of satan and His demons, the sin in the Garden of Eden, or the day we decided to make God the Lord of our lives.
4. To whom much has been given, much is required.

While each of these is an imperative for each believer to remind him or herself daily, pay particular attention to number five which provides believers with a grave reminder that not only have we been given much, but God is also REQUIRING a divine return upon his investment in each one of us. That is, if He has invested the gifts of prophecy in you, He expects you to prophesy His word. If He has invested His gift of healing, then He expects you to lay hands on the sick in Jesus name and watch them by the power of the Holy Ghost manifest miraculous recoveries. If He invested the gift of preaching or teaching or whatever in you, He has done so for His reason and for His kingdom's purpose, and He expects you to exercise His investment in you while you are here, so that when you return to Him and give ACCOUNT for what you have done with His investment in you He will be satisfied and say unto you "Well done my good and faithful servant."

We should never allow the teaching of I Corinthians 4:1-2 to escape our hearts. These particular verses remind us that ". . . men ought to regard us as servants of Christ, and those entrusted with the secret things of God. Now it is REQUIRED (you are accountable) that those who have been given a trust MUST PROVE FAITHFUL (at the time of their accounting to God.)"

And because of this, according to Romans 14:12, ". . . each of us WILL GIVE an account of himself to God." In other words, because God has individually, uniquely, and completely equipped each of us to perform a particular mission in this earth realm, which ONLY we can perform, we must in turn account to the Master for our obedience and willingness to do what we were created, called, predestined, equipped and sent forth to do, or account to Him for our disobedience, rebelliousness, and unfaithfulness. The choice is ours, but then so is the corresponding reward.

Exactly What Is Accounting To God?

Still, what does giving an account actually mean? To give is to render, provide, submit or to offer up. Account (biblically) refers to rendering testimony to, personal acceptance of, or confirming responsibility for every deed, thought, behavior, decision, act, or word we gave birth to while serving in this earth realm. Giving account of our life refers to standing in the very presence of God and individually and privately accepting total spiritual responsibility for every seen and unseen, every heard and unheard, every shared and secret, every public and private, every righteous and sinful thought, word, desire, deed, motivation or intent we have permitted to become part of our character, spirit and existence.

Daniel 5:27 explains the consequences of not enforcing high (stewardship) morals over these areas of our lives: "Tekel: You have been weighed in the balance and are found wanting." By this God (through Daniel the writer) warns us thusly: I made you my servant, my witness, my ambassador. I gave you my power and anointing. I gave you my strength, my image and my likeness. I protected you with my angels. I gave you my son. I taught you my will. I sent you my Holy Ghost. Then I entrusted you with my secrets. And now after you've deserted your sanctified mission, left your first love, followed the bewitching voice of another, and now here you stand on My divine scales of righteous having to ACCOUNT to me for all you've done. But God is also saying that according to the divine ACCOUNTING SCALES, when He told you to step onto them so that he could weigh your faithfulness verses you unfaithful, so that He can weigh your obedience verses your rebelliousness, so that He can weigh you belief verses your doubt, so that He can weigh your commitment verses your slouthfulness, so that He could weigh your righteous motivation verses you selfish motives, so that He could weigh the Word that was operating in you verses the intellect that controlled you, He says He finds you wanting. In other words God says in-spite of having sung in the choir, by His standards He finds you deficient. In spite of being called a prophet, He says he finds you missing the mark. In spite of speaking in tongues and shouting and quoting scriptures, He says He finds your spiritual account to be deplete and totally insufficient to earn the kingdom's greatest rewards. He is saying that now that your moment of accountability is here, a meticulous and in-depth spiritual review of your life and deeds as you stand before naked on the scales of eternity has revealed that your faith was too circumstantial, your obedience too sporadic., your praise and worship too scripted, prepared, and rehearsed. Your shouts of joy and joyful noises were never rendered. Your love was too selective. Your prayer and fasting were done only during periods of convenience. And as a result, His judgment sentence for such a person shall be "Depart from Me you worker of iniquity. I never knew you."

It's Your Choice—It's Your Eternity

Godly accountability. No man, woman, boy, or girl alive will be able to escape it. John said he ". . . saw the great and the small" giving account unto God. Whatever you do, no matter the cost, never, ever let your heavenly account become delinquent nor deficient because verily I say unto you, surely the day SHALL come when each of us will have to individually and personally give a full ACCOUNTABILITY of our lives to God Himself. What will you hear Him say when YOU step onto His scales of accountability?

Blessings.

Praise God from whom all blessings flow! Praise Him all creatures here below. Praise Him above the heavenly host! Praise Father, Son and Holy Ghost!

Praise is comely before the Lord.

GOD, YOU ARE ONE BA-A-ADD DUDE!!

Y'all forgive me for saying it this way, but I know of no more accurate or any truer way to give God the glory than to just straight out say it like this, GOD, YOU ARE ONE B-A-A-A-D DUDE!! Sure theologians would express their admiration more appropriately. And bishops and pastors would perhaps use more sanctimonious terms. The scholars would, no doubt, express their awe of the King, in a more erudite fashion. But I, as one who truly knows that I am Your handiwork, I'm Your offspring, I'm the object of Your love, I'm the reason and justification for the holes that are still on display in glory and the purpose for which You came, bled and died, I have no problem saying it and saying it out loud . . . when I read and look upon Your creation, I cannot help but to marvel and to proclaim that You, **God, are ONE BAD DUDE!!**

You started creation off with a demonstration of just how awesomely BADDD You are! For when I read that "In the beginning," when there was nobody or nothing else—when you autonomously and sovereignly decided that You'd produce a creation. Thus, the fourth word of the beginnings is "GOD"! Why? Because in the beginning there was nothing BUT God. There were no counsels. There were no institutions. There were no organizations. There were no committees. There were no boards. In the beginning there was NOTHING BUT GOD! (And note that word **nothing,** because we're coming back to it soon.) And it was THIS GOD and this God alone who created the heavens and the earth. But we should not read over that too quickly because if we do, we'll miss out on something this very important there. You didn't make or shape or form or fashion. God you **created**. In other words you brought into existence out of NOTHING—everything that is! You stepped out on NOTHING! You saw NOTHING! You spoke into NOTHING! You gave a command to NOTHING! And command it by the word of your power to bring forth every utterance of Your speech and desire of Your mind and heart. NOW THAT'S A BAD DUDE!! In other words You're so bad that the only thing it took for You to build everything was Your word and Your own inherent power . . . and NOTHING else.

Who else could have stood on NOTHING? (Remembering that the very word nothing means not a thing. Not a floating speck of dust. Not a single cell creature. Not a flash of light. Not a single thing. You, with your bad self, defied all logic, reason, and know how and stood on absolutely nothing and uttered a command that out of NOTHING everything thing was to come forth. And here is how we KNOW you're bad. Because you didn't just say it . . . but what You said You saw and, today you have left it on display in the firmaments that we may gaze upon the same creations that You gazed upon at the time of creation and commented that they were good.

And then the next few verses go on to tell us "And God Said, 'Let there be . . . '." Question? Who were You talking to? There was nobody else around when You created all that there is. Whom were You telling to let these things be? The answer: Your own POWER. Not only do you have inherent and unmatchable powers, but You and You alone exercise full control of them. (That is why if You are on our side WHO can stand against us?) And it all started from NOTHING. Who in his right natural mind would speak into nothing and not just expect to **GET** what he was bold enough to speak? Who could have done that except you, God? Whom? Certainly no power less grand and magnificent than Yours could have caused such to be. I say again . . . God . . . you are one BAAAAD DUDE!!

But You didn't stop there. To show us just how much the creation stands in awe and recognition of You and Your sovereignty over it, even though You called all things into existence out of nothing, once they arrived on the scene, they didn't begin to do their own thing and decide upon their own duties and responsibilities. NO! The seas came forth and remained empty until You commanded them to produce the fish and the creatures of the seas and all that inhabit them. The skies didn't set their own course of duty. Rather, they remained empty until You filled them with the foul and the birds. The trees and nature stood at the position of attention until You gave the sun it's order to serve as the greater light and the moon its order to serve as the lesser light. The trees, the fruits, the beasts of the fields stood fast until You instructed them to reproduce after their own kinds and to bring forth only after their own kind. Now that's a BAAAADDD DUDE that can speak into nothing, talk to trees, give orders to naked water and command nature—and it all obeys! Say what you want, but from my perspective—That's One BAAAADDD DUDE!

And then You took the dust, that which cannot even assume a solid form or shape, yet You shaped it into Your own image and commanded it to hold fast to its assigned form—and it did. Then You breath into the lump of dust, Your own breath of life. And that which was the equivalent of a lifeless body suddenly was awaken by Your power of Your presence within it and Your grace and became a living, thinking, functioning, in-the-image-of-God being. God, you're awesome plus some! Oh yeah, and you're a BAAAADDD DUDE too!

But what I like most about Your awesomeness is how great of a teacher You are. In Genesis (the beginnings) Chapter 1, You lovingly teach us through Your word that You are the creator of all things. That is why You purposely anointed Your writer to refer to You as God, meaning the creator and sustainer of all things. And the writer continues to refer to You as such until he reaches Genesis 2:4 where he changes his references to You to read "The Lord God" meaning the rightful and legal owner of all that He has created and sustains. (Lord literally means the one who is the rightful owner/overseer. God, synonymous with El Shadai or El Elyon or the one who is the creator and upholder of all things by the word of His power).

You created all that there is from nothing but Your own vision and by Your own power. That is why You are the legal LORD of all things. You are the divine entity who caused all that is to be; that is why You are the God of gods and the Lord of lords. You uphold and sustain Your creation by the word of Your power, that is power is an inherent facet of Your makeup and whatever You want to happen You simply register the desires of Your heart upon your undefeatable words and You send them forth—even into nothingness—riding upon Your inherent power never to return unto You void. God, only a BADDD DUDE could do that!

And if that's were enough, You left the Genesis and gave us a history lesson of the future. You gave us a revelation (the book of Revelations) that no natural eye, mouth or mind could have shared with us. Recalling that the word revelation literally means "a shared truth" I am reminded that You taught us that "I am the way, THE TRUTH . . . ." Therefore, a revelation is not just a clearer picture, rather, it is You sharing or giving us a deeper insight into You and all things that are TRUTH.

You started us in the beginnings and took us to the tomorrow which has no tomorrow! All with accuracy. All with power. All with clarity. And all because You're not just our creator and sustainer, but because You're our Father who art in heaven. You're our savior. You're our keeper. You're our comforter. You're our peace. You're our hope for eternity. You're our confidence for today. And so much more, God, because without apology or debate, we boldly confess before every demon in hell and in the presence and company of every angel in heaven that YOU GOD ARE ONE BAAAADDDD DUDE! There is none like You. There is no equal. There is no peer. There is no rival. There is only YOU and You alone. And YOU, God . . . you are ONE BA-A-A-A-D-D-D-D DUDE!!!

Blessings.

We are receivers by design. God is our supernatural transmitter and orders giver by His own nature and will. If we would simply receive what God transmits to us, we would easily recognize our majestic powers to bring heaven to earth.

The Truth About the Active
and the Passive Voices

Years ago—many years ago—I was a fledging undergraduate student. And, of course, as most college curricula are designed, freshmen are mandated to take the one course they all hate—literature and composition, or what we commonly call English 101. And what is so difficult about the course is not the composition and analysis portion, but, the writing or composition portion. Students painstakingly record their thoughts, arguments, beliefs and analysis and submit them in neatly typed papers to their instructors only to have them returned with enough red ink on them to perform a blood transfusion.

In most cases students will discover that the reason for the bleeding is either due to syntax, mechanics, grammar or usage errors, or writing in the passive rather than the active voice. And this, the active and passive voices, is what I'd like to teach on in this writing.

First of all, let us remember that Jesus said that He wished to teach us spiritual things, but if we could not first understand the natural, how, then would we understand the spiritual? And if we do not understand the spiritual, how, then can we apply it and receive manifestation from it? So, from the outset, allow me to say that I am only using a natural concept in order to illuminate and teach a spiritual principal. So stick with me as we go through this one.

Linguistically speaking, the active and passive voices of nearly all languages can be easily confused and misapplied, even in your heavenly language. It is vital that you know and correct this for this simple reason. It is the active voice which causes or brings about an event, a condition, an action or an occurrence. It is the active voice which makes a thing happen or makes it so or makes it become. On the other hand, it is the passive voice which is acted upon by the passive voice. The active voice "decrees" a thing into existence and the passive voice "believes and receives" whatever the active voice has decreed into existence or reality. It is the active voice which causes and the passive voice which receives. Nothing becomes until or unless it is brought about by the active voice. And nothing is realized until it is received by the passive voice. In other words the active voice "ACTS" upon the passive voice and the passive voice "BECOMES" what the active voices decrees. Now follow me.

GOD IS OUR ACTIVE VOICE AND WE ARE HIS PASSIVE SERVANTS, INSTRUMENTS AND CHILDREN. God is the voice which decrees what is truth about and over us. Then through faith, we, his passive children, believe, receive and apply the truth of what God has said about us to lives. For, just as He told Jeremiah, I knew you before I formed you in the womb and I declared you a prophet unto the nations. The fact that Jeremiah became a mighty prophet for the Kingdom of God was not news to God, He had already decreed it to be so in Jeremiah's life—before there was a Jeremiah for it to be so over. God Himself ACTED upon and activated certain destinies in the life of Jeremiah before Jeremiah ever existed. Then upon his arrival into the earth and physical realm, Jeremiah believed and received the word of God about him and applied God's declarations to his life and the word that God had ordained to transform Jeremiah from an average to a mighty person then had a legal access and right to cause what the ACTIVE VOICE had decreed to BECOME real in the earth realm in the form of Jeremiah.

But God didn't stop with Jeremiah. GOD has decreed many things over and about each one of us as well. The problem is not that GOD is no longer decreeing. The problem is we are no longer receiving. We are no longer believing. We are no longer applying. We are no longer obeying.

We must understand this simple concept. When we receive what God has said about us, we don't question it. We don't ponder it. We don't try to make it make sense to us. We don't ask why? And we don't trying to run a spiritual miracle through a natural mind. For we know that the natural mind is enemy to God and that it cannot understand the ways and teachings of the Holy Spirit. Now let's put ourselves to the test.

When God says, "You have been made the righteousness of God" why do we question it? Why can't we just thank God for choosing us, and blessing us, and selecting us, and saving us? Why must He now justify to us? We do it, because we are yet unable or unwilling to accept what the active voice has done for us. And so we continue to walk around depressed, defeated and powerless. It's not because God would have you to be that way. It's because you are not able to accept what He has decreed over you!

When God has said that you are no more servants but friends, why can't we believe it? He's already decreed it (activated the relationship) over you. Now why do you, by way of your doubt and faithlessness, keep calling Him a liar?

When God has said that you are the salt of the earth, why do you keep looking at your mistakes and saying "I know He wasn't talking about me" instead of looking to your Savior and Redeemer and saying "God, in-spite of my imperfections, weakness and missteps, I thank you for gracing me to be your salt in the eyes of men here on earth"?

Listen to me, brothers and sisters. The Bible says that the word of God is active and alive. It also teaches us that the word of God will not go forth and return unto Him void, but will accomplish that to which God sent it. Does this mean that the Word (which is God in spoken form), will convert you against your own will? No!

You must ALLOW or permit the word of God to enter into your heart and to rule you from the inside out.

The word of God convicts us of our sins. Then we yield to the conviction and He convinces us that there is a better way for us. We agree to the conviction and we yield ourselves over to the powers and graces of God and there, by faith, He converts us from sinners to children and cancels our past deeds. Then He covers us in his love and grace and calls us his sons and daughters.

Now think about it. Did you convict yourself? No! You were active upon by the convicting powers of our active voice. Did you convince yourself. No. You were convinced by the Holy Ghost. Did you become saved by your own doing? Did you decide on your own that you would be called a son or daughter? No. It was done BY the active voice on your behalf. Did you convert yourself? No. Your spirit was acted upon and converted by God.

It is God who is our active voice. Why can't we be His obedient passive and obedient children and just say, "Daddy, I don't understand it. I don't even know why You chose me. But, just as Mary said to the angel Gabriel, 'Be it unto me'."

You didn't cause yourself to be saved. You are saved BY grace through faith. This means that there is a force or source outside of you that is responsible for acting upon you and causing or decreeing events to manifest in your life. You didn't grace yourself. God acted upon your life and caused it to be. You didn't keep or protect yourself. You didn't regenerate your own spirit. You didn't cause angels to be encamped round about you. God activated all of these things in your life for you. Why can't you believe and receive them?

If God says (and He does) that you are filled with the wisdom of God because Jesus has made unto me wisdom, righteousness, sanctification and redemption then STOP arguing with Him and begin to thank Him for what He has already made available unto you "according to your (own) faith"!

Believe in the Word of God! Then you will begin to see the things God has already done for you before you even asked Him. Stop walking around acting as if you're some weakling or spineless, lost or confused thing. You are the voice of God in action. Stop letting your bleak yesterdays deprive you of your powerful tomorrows. Why wouldn't you do this? Look at what God has activated over you:

> I have put off the old man and put on the new man which is renewed in the knowledge after the image of Him who created me and I have received the Spirit of Wisdom and Revelation in the knowledge of Him. The eyes of my understanding are being divinely enlightened. I am not conformed to this world, but I am transformed y the renewing of my mind. My mind is renewed by the Word of God! I am strengthen with all might according to His glorious power. I am delivered from the power of darkness and I am translated into the kingdom of His Dear Son. I am born of God and I have world overcoming faith residing on the inside of me. Much greater is He that is in me than he that is in the world. I can do all things through Christ Jesus who strengthens me.

These words were not left to us just for our reading pleasure. This is a decree that has been activated over you, your life, your situation and even your eternity. All that remains is for you to believe, receive and apply the truth of God's every word to your situations.

If you're still questioning God's word, then you have not yet come to accept Him as Your savior. You must BELIEVE God in order to accept God. You will never accept God as the God of your life if you do not first believe that He is everything He has said in His word. He is not a partial savior, redeemer, provider, protector, father or God. HE IS!! Not a part . . . not a percentage . . . not a piece. HE IS.

We must decide to trust Him in-spite of our natural confusion. As I said earlier, Mary was confused as she spoke with the angel Gabriel. She even questioned him. (How can this thing be as I have not known a man?) She did not understand how what God said about her could be so in the natural. Yet in her spirit she received and acted upon the word of God ("Be it unto me according to your words").

That's where God is trying to get us to. He's trying to get us to a place where we will simply say, "Be it unto me according to Your word, God". In other words, You have said it and that's makes it true and enough for me. I don't know how? I don't know when? I don't know why? I don't know where. But, thanks be to YOU, I do know THAT!! I know that you said it. I know that you decreed it. I know that you hasten to perform your word. I know that whatever you have decreed over me is my purpose, power, destiny, and place. So I won't argue any more. I won't debate anymore. I won't discuss or contemplate anymore. I'll just receive whatever You have said about me . . . because that is what is true about and for my life.

God is our active voice. We are His passive receivers. He works through us as a result of our obedience and faith.

Is God really the active voice of your life? Think about it. "My sheep know my voice and the voice of another they will not obey."

Who's activating things in your life?

Thank You, Father. Thank You for activating YOURSELF within this earthen vessel. Thank You for activating agape love, perpetual forgiveness, continual compassion, a fearlessly faithful spirit and a hunger for holiness within my inner man. For I could never have done this myself. But You, God, spoke it over and about me and activated the attributes of Your divine and majestic self in my spirit that I may be a righteous representative of Christ Jesus here on earth. Thank You for your active voice and thank You for my receptive passive spirit. Amen, God, Amen! Blessings.

You'll never see all that God has
for you until you decide to do <u>all</u>
that He has commanded of you.

N-O-W Lift Up Thine Eyes . . .

[Genesis 12:1-5] Now the Lord had said unto Abram, Get thee out of thy country, and from thy kindred, and from thy father's house, unto a land that I sill shew thee: And I will make of thee a great nation, and I will bless thee, and make thy name great; and thou shalt be a blessing. And I will bless them that bless thee and curse him that curseth thee; and in thee shall all families of the earth be blessed. So Abram departed, as the Lord had spoken unto him; and Lot went with him: and Abram was seventy five years old when he departed out of Haran. And Abram took Sarai his wife, and Lot his brother's son . . ."

Many believers will not accept as truth, that it is their partial obedience that stops the fullness of God from operating in their lives. They are totally ignorant to the fact that partial obedience is full disobedience in the eyes of God. When God has promised you something, it's a done deal. For all of his promises ARE—not shall become—not can be—not will materialize—but all promises of God ARE yes and AMEN!

Why, then, doesn't every believer see the results of the promises? In most cases, it is because we choose to obey God only to the extent that we choose, understand or are comfortable. This is called partial obedience or more accurately FULL DISOBEDIENCE. And it is the "DIS" portion of the word that stops you from receiving the fullness of what God has spoken into your spirit.

"DIS" is a prefix which mean "NOT". So if we are walking in DISobedience we are NOT walking in obedience which automatically takes us out of the will and the provisions of God. Let me give you a Biblical example of what I'm saying.

Please read the above scripture. Notice that God gave Abram SPECIFIC instructions: 1) Get the out of thy country and 2) Get from around your kin folks. 3) Get out of they father's house. 4) And go to a place where I will lead and guide you. Why? (Here comes the word of promise.) Because I have something for you. I have greatness awaiting you there. I have your destiny on hold in that place. It is where your anointing will be made manifest. It is where your provisions are. It is where you are not only transformed, but you will transform the lives of others. It is where I transform you from what you see into what I see you as. It is where you grow up in me. It is where you learn to hear my voice, heed my word and submit to my will. But (God is saying) I have put it all on reserve for you in a specific place which you can reach only by way of obedience to my instructions.

Observe carefully what God said to Abram: *"Now the Lord had said unto Abram, Get thee out of thy country, and from thy kindred, and from thy father's house, unto a land that I sill shew thee: And I will make of thee a great nation, and I will bless thee, and make thy name great; and thou shalt be a blessing. And I will bless them that bless thee and curse him that curseth thee; and in thee shall all families of the earth be blessed.*

God told Abram that if he would just leave his country (area of familiarity and comfort), and leave his kindred (cousins, friends, acquaintances and colleagues) and get away from his father's house (the area he regarded as his home) and trust Him (God) to lead him to a place, a location, a height, a success, a plateau, a level of achievement and recognition that he (Abram) had not only never known, but had never dreamed, asked or imagined. And then God takes it a step further by telling Abram that if YOU will trust ME to do this great thing for you, not only will I do just that—BUT—I will make sure that your greatness is indeed too great just for you and your family. I'll endow you with greatness to the extent that you will share it with your off springs and make them great and they with theirs and make them great and they with theirs and make them great and so on and so on. In other words the level of greatness that I will bestow upon you is only coming through you, but is too much just for you. It is greatness for many. It is power form many. It is anointing for many. I'm just using you to get it into the earth realm. It is not only for you, it is for those who will come after you. It is for those whom you will never know or see. This level of greatness is for a nation and not a person. I've just asked you—the person—to allow me—the creator—to use your vessel to release my glory into the earth realm and over the lives of many. But I can't do it until you move away from your country, from your present location, from your friends, from your acquaintances, from your current situation, from your present job, from your present hesitations. Once you move THEN I can show you the greatness I have for you. Let's prove this Biblically:

> *(Genesis 13:2-18): And Abram went up out of Egypt, he and his wife, and all that he had, and Lot with him, into the south. And Abram was very rich in cattle, in silver, and in gold. And he went on his journeys from the south even to Bethel, unto the place where his tent had been at the beginning, between Bethel and Hai, Unto the place of the alter, which he had made there at the first: and there Abram called on the name of the Lord. And Lot also, which went with Abram, had flocks, and herds, and tents. And the land was not able to bear them, that they might dwell together: for their substance was great, so that they could not dwell together. And there was a strife between the herdmen of Abram's cattle and the herdmen of Lort's cattle. And the Canaanite and the Perizzite dwelled then in the land. And Abram said unto Lot, Let there be no strife, I pray thee, between me and thee, and between my herdmen and thy herdmen, for we be brethren. Is not the whole land before*

thee? Separate theyself, I pray theee, from me; if though wilt take the left hand, then I will go to the right; or if thou depart to the right hand, then I will go to the left. And Lot lifted up his eyes, and beheld all the plain of Jordan that it was well watered everywhere, before the Lord destroyed Sodom and Gomorrah, even as the garden of the Lord, like the land of Egypt, as thou comest unto Zoar. Then Lot chose him all the plain of Jordan; and Lot journeyed east; and they separated themselves the one from the other. Abram dwelled in the land of Cannan, and Lot dwelled in the cities of the plain, and pitched his tent toward Sodom. But the men of Sodom were wicked and sinners before the Lord exceedingly. And the Lord said unto Abram, after that Lot was separated from him, Lift up now thine eyes, and look form the place where thou art northward, and southward and eastward and westward: For all the land which thou seest, to thee will I give it, and to thy seed for ever. And I will make thy seed as the dust of the earth; so that if a man can number the dust of the earth, then shall they seed also be numbered. Arise, walk through the land in the length of it and in the breath of it; for I will give it unto thee. Then Abram removed his tent, and came and dwelt in the plain of Mamre, which is in Hebron, and built there an alter unto the Lord."

The specific instructions had already been given by God to Abram. And so had the Word of promise. However, Abram only PARTIALLY obeyed God. God told him to leave his kindred, but Abram didn't. Now when God spoke of kindred he was not referring to Abram's wife, as God has told us in his own word that whom God has put together let no man (or himself) put asunder (or cause to break up). Further, he told us that "Then shall a man leave his father and his mother and CLEAVE unto his wife and they shall be one flesh." This is very important because we need to know that God sees (Godly) husbands and wives as ONE and not two separate individuals. Therefore, when God told Abram to leave his kindred his wife is not considered a kindred, but as an intricate part (helpmeet) of her husband.

But Lot was not! Lot was Abram's nephew whose father had been loyal to Abram and had died. Abram had taken his brother's son into his house to raise him as his own. But God told Abram to get from around his kindred! Yes, Abram meant well, but he was still walking in disobedience. And since God's word is forever settled in heaven, God could not release into Abram's life all that he had for him. Therefore God allowed Lot himself to show Abram why God wanted them separated.

Abram was rich. So rich that he actually had an overflow of riches and his nephew had profited from Abram's overflow. He profited so much until he began to believe that it was by his own abilities that his herds grew. But in actuality the blessing was upon and for Abram, but the overflow was for those in the vicinity. Lot's arrogance clearly defines the condition of his heart as he challenges his older and wiser uncle. He told him (through his herdsmen) that there no longer was room for both his and his uncle's herds to graze together. His herdsmen had actually begun to fight with those of Abram, the man who had taken him into his own home and raised him as his own.

But Abram did not fight with him. Instead he told his nephew to look around and to decided in which direction he would like to take his herd, and whatever direction he did not take, that would be the direction he (Abram) would take. Lot looked about and took what looked like the best possible grazing and watering spot. So he took his men, his herd and his himself and departed.

But herein is the beauty of the word and promises of God. Once Lot departed, Abram was THEN walking in obedience. He was out of his country. He was out of his father's house. He was headed to a place where God had led him. And he was no longer around his kindred. Now look at what God says to him (as soon as Lot had left!): "And the Lord said unto Abram, after that Lot was separated from him, Lift up NOW thine eyes, and look form the place where thou art northward, and southward and eastward and westward: For all the land which thou seest, to thee will I give it, and to thy seed for ever. And I will make thy seed as the dust of the earth."

Note the word NOW. He never told him to lift up his eyes and look from where he was until he was walking in TOTAL OBEDIENCE. Could he have shown him the promise before? Sure he could have. But did he do it. No? Why? Because God will never reveal all that he has for you while you are walking contrary to his will and instructions. **Now**, Abram, that you are in compliance with my instructions! **Now**, Abram, that you are following my will for you! **Now**, Abram, that you are trusting my word and my ways and leaning not to your own understanding. **Now**, Abram, that you are honoring my word above your own intellect and rationalization! **N-O-W** you can look up from where you are. You don't have to go any place else. I don't have to carry you to any other spot. I don't need to relocate you to reveal unto you. **NOW** you can look up from where you are and see the glory that I have prepared for you.

Now comes the beautiful part. It's not just for you, Abram. This glory is too much just for you. I've released enough glory in this single blessing that you can pass it from generation to generation to generation.

I know Lot may have gone in a direction. But once Abram walks upon it and claims it, God has decreed that it's his too! *"Arise, walk through the land in the length of it and in the breath of it; for I will give it unto thee. For all the land which thou seest, to thee will I give it, and to thy seed . . . ."*

What am I saying? I'm asking you just how many times have you blocked God's anointing, grace and blessings from FULLY manifesting in your life because you have chosen to operate in partial obedience or full disobedience. God will not release all he has until you release all that you are holding on to, believe in, counting on, and trusting in. What is the Lot in your life? And of what promise are you robbing youself? You can't take everybody with you, people! But if you want to go to that place where **your** greatness is being secured and maintained just for you, let go of your Lot and take a hold of God through your full obedience to His Word. And then, watch God say to you . . .

N-O-W lift up thine eyes from the very place where you are right now and behold all that I have for you!

Blessings.

A Pause to Bless Him

COUNT YOUR BLESSINGS

When upon life's billows you are tempest tossed,
When you are discouraged, thinking all is lost,
Count your many blessings, name them one by one,
And it will surprise you what the Lord hath done.

Refrain

Count your blessings, name them one by one,
Count your blessings, see what God hath done!
Count your blessings, name them one by one,
And it will surprise you what the Lord hath done.

Are you ever burdened with a load of care?
Does the cross seem heavy you are called to bear?
Count your many blessings, every doubt will fly,
And you will keep singing as the days go by.

Refrain

When you look at others with their lands and gold,
Think that Christ has promised you His wealth untold;
Count your many blessings. Wealth can never buy
Your reward in heaven, nor your home on high.

Refrain

So, amid the conflict whether great or small,
Do not be disheartened, God is over all;
Count your many blessings, angels will attend,
Help and comfort give you to your journey's end.

Twenty-five Reasons to Continue the Fight

1. I AM MADE IN THE IMAGE AND THE LIKENESS OF THE ONE AND ONLY TRUE AND ETERNAL GOD.
2. I FELL FROM GLORY DUE TO THE SIN OF THE FIRST ADAM.
3. I WAS RESCUED FROM MY SINFUL STATE BY CHRIST THE SECOND AND LAST ADAM.
4. I HAVE ACCEPTED GOD AS MY FATHER AND HIS SON JESUS CHRIST AS MY MESSIAH AND SAVIOR.
5. I AM A SAVED, SANTIFIED, REBORN CHILD OF THE MOST HIGH GOD.
6. MY BIG BROTHER AND SAVIOR, JESUS CHRIST, TRIUMPHED OVER EVERY EVIL THNG, POWER, PRINCIPALITY, RULER AND SPIRIT OF THE KINGDOM OF DARKNESS FOR ME.
7. JESUS CHRIST ROSE AND MADE AN OPEN MOCKERY OF THE WORKS OF THE DEVIL AND THE KINGDOM OF DARKNESS. HE ALREADY RENDERED THEM HARMLESS AND INEFFECTIVE AGAINST ME.

8. JESUS CHRIST LEFT ME HIS POWER AND GAVE ME THE AUTHORITY TO USE IT IN THE EARTH REALM.

9. JESUS CHRIST NOW SITS AT THE RIGHT HAND OF THE FATHER.

10. BECAUSE I AM A CHILD OF THE MOST HIGH; AND BECAUSE JESUS IS MY SAVIOR AND GOD IS MY FATHER, I, IN THE SPIRT REALM, NOW SIT WITH MY BROTHER JESUS CHIRST IN HEAVENLY PLACES AT THE RIGHT HAND OF THE FATHER.

11. I AM THE RIGHTEOUS OF GOD.

12. THERE IS THEREFORE NOW NO CONDEMNATION OF ME BY ANY MAN, WOMAN OR PERSON BECAUSE OF MY LOVE FOR, ACCEPTANCE OF AND OBEDIENCE TO THE FATHER.

13. NOTHING CAN DEFEAT ME.

14. NOTHING IS GREATER THAN THE POWER THAT LIVES IN ME.

15. NOTHING SHALL BY ANY MEAN OVERPOWER, OVERTAKE, DECEIVE, PERSUADE, COAX OR DRAW ME OUT OF THE HAND OF THE FATHER.

16. I AM DESTINED TO SPEND ETERNITY IN GLORY WITH GOD THE FATHER AND JESUS THE SAVIOR.

17. I WILL LIVE IN NEW JERUSALEM WHICH IS THE RE-CREATED GARDEN OF EDEN GIVEN TO MAN AGAIN THAT THE UNWAVERING WILL, PURPOSE AND INTENTION OF GOD MY BE FULFILLED AS ORIGINALLY PLANNED AND PRE-DESTINED.

18. I HAVE HOLY GHOST POWER. I HAVE SUPERNATURAL WISDOM. I HAVE GOD-ORDAINED AUTHORITY. AND I AM A SANCTIFIED, HOLY GHOST EMPOWERED TOOL

FOR THE KINGDOM OF GOD AND AGAINST THE KINGDOM OF DARKNESS.

19. AND ALL OF THESE THINGS AND MORE ARE FOUND AND ARE TRUE IN THE WORD OF GOD. AND SINCE THE WORD OF GOD IS IN ME, THAT MEANS, EVERY ONE OF THESE WORDS AND ITS CORRESPONDING TRUTH IS ALSO FOUND IN ME.

20. AND SO TODAY, THIS, MOMENT, THIS SECOND, RIGHT NOW, WHERE I STAND BECAUSE I KNOW THIS TO BE TRUE, BECAUSE I RECEIVE THE TRUTH OF THESE WORDS IN MY SPIRIT MAN; BECAUSE BY FAITH I CONFESS EVERY ONE OF THEM OVER MY OWN LIFE AND MY FAMILY'S LIFE TODAY!! RIGHT NOW!!! NOT ANOTHER MINUTE FROM NOW. NOT ANOTHER SECOND FROM NOW. BUT RIGHT NOW!!! I—BY FAITH AND THE HOLY GHOST POWER GIVEN TO ME AS A PROMISE FROM THE FATHER—I BOLDLY STAND AND RECKON EACH ONE OF THESE CONFESSIONS TO BE ALIVE, ACTIVE, REAL, TRUE AND AN OPERATING PART OF ME FROM THIS VERY SECOND UNTIL THE SECOND THAT I DIE AND AM RAISED AGAIN OR UNTIL I AM RAPTURED OUT OF THIS SINFUL WORLD.

21. I'M BLESSED. I'M SUPERNATUREALLY EMPOWERED. I'M SAVED. I'M CONFIDENT. I'M RIGHTEOUSLY BOLD. AND I'M A WARRIOR AGAINS ALL THAT IS UNHOLY.

22. FOR I HAVE BEEN GIVEN THIS POWER, THIS ANOINTING, THIS CHARGE, THIS GRACE, THIS AUTHORITY BY THE ONE AND ONLY LIVING JEHOVAH, EL SHADAI, YAWAH AND GOD ALMIGHTY AND NEVER AGAIN WILL I FRUSTRATE AND DISAPPOINT HIM BY NOT WALKING IN THE AUTHORITY HE HAS

GRANTED, GRACED, AUTHORIZED, ORDAINED AND LOOSED IN MY LIFE.

23. I PROFESS THIS. I CONFESS THIS. I RECEIVE THIS. I BELIEVE THIS. I ACTIVATE THIS. AND THIS DAY, THIS MOMENT, I RECKON IT TO BE SO, REAL, AND TRUE IN EVERY ASPECT OF MY LIFE AND IN ALL THAT MAKES ME UP AS A PERSON AND AS A SPIRIT.

24. AND SO I SAY TO THE DEVIL. DEVIL, TAKE YOUR RIGHTFUL PLACE. THAT PLACE IS BENEATH ME. THAT PLACE IS BEHIND ME. THAT PLACE IS UNDER MY FEET. FOR NOTHING THAT YOU PLAN, PLOT OR DEVISE CAN SUCCEED AGAINST ME HENCEFORTH.

25. THIS AND EVERY WORD THAT GOD HAS SAID ABOUT ME IN HIS HOLY BIBLE AND EVEN IN THE PRIVACY OF MY OWN SPIRIT MAN, I BELIEVE, RECEIVE, AND RECKON IT TO BE SO RIGHT NOW. AMEN.

Now Behold the Lamb

Now behold the precious Lamb of God

The perfect sacrifice who came to take away my sin

The propitiation for my imperfection, rebelliousness and waywardness

The only one justified, qualified and worthy to open the seal of the Lamb's Book of Life

Now behold He who was from the beginning

Now behold Him who presently is

Behold Him who was

Behold Him who cannot cannot be

Behold The Word of God Incarnate

Behold The Great I Am

Behold Divine Promise as a flesh and blood man

Behold ancient Prophecy as modern person

Behold strength as meakness

And King as Servant

Behold infinity made into finiteness

Behold Alpha and Omega personified

Behold fault and perfection

Behold divinity and mankind

Behold sin and glory

Behold the father, the son and the Spirit in one

Behold the sinner and the savior

Behold the dead and the risen

Behold the cursed and the praised

Behold the smitten and the healer

Behold the warrior and the bringer of every lasting peace

Behold the past and the present and the future in one

Behold He and He alone who is the perfected Lamb of God

Chosen and slain before the foundation of the earth

Now . . . behold the Lamb of God!!

ONLY GOD IS THE WAY, <u>THE TRUTH</u> AND THE LIFE

My wife and I took a short vacation, hopped a plane with a couple of friends and headed off to Korea to do some shopping. We later took another vacation, hopped another plane and headed to China to do some sightseeing, and, oh yes, some shopping. A few months ago we visited Cambodia and Viet Nam where once again my wife pulled into every market we passed where we did what? You got it. Some shopping. A couple of years ago, while attending a training in San Diego, a small group of us decided to cross the border and go into Mexico to do, what else, more shopping. In a few months we will head to Thailand where we will eat, sightsee and, once more, shop.

But herein lies the lesson that all of this shopping has taught me—that everybody wants a deal. Everybody wants the best, the most beautiful, the ideal, the perfect and the most, but we all want to pay as little as possible for it. We want the best that life has to offer, but we don't want to pay what the best actually costs. And so as I travel around the world, what I have become keenly aware of is that the market for "FAKES," "IMMITATIONS," AND "LOOK ALIKES" is huge and growing larger everyday. Oddly enough, there are some people who boldly confess that they aren't even looking for "the real thing" because it costs too much.

These people admit that what they are looking for is something that resembles that which is real. They don't want a Rolex, but a Rolex look-a-like. They don't want a Coach or Tag or any other brand name item, because it costs too much for them to wear the real thing. So they go bargain hunting. And the merchants know this. So there are shops set up to accommodate these appetites for the fakes, imitations and look-a-likes. The market is huge. And the profit to the vendors is even more huge. But the customers continue to swarm the shops, demanding the knock-offs at the discounted prices. And then, self absorbed in their newly acquired imitations they parade them about proudly and ostentatiously as if to advertise to unsuspecting admirers that which is neither real or of any significant value.

Thus, as believers we must come to know that there is a master merchant of discounted faith, discontinued trust, marked down devotion, special deal on prayers, and blue light special obedience. His name is Satan and he is the master marketer. While he is unable to replicate the anointing or the Grace of God to do the Father's will, he is a master disguiser of wickedness, corruption, evil, deception, weakness, ignorance, rebellion and disobedience. Simply put, there is nothing that is genuine in the spirit realm which he has not sought to pervert and to imitate. He imitates preaching. He imitates praying. He imitates worship, He imitates thanksgiving. He imitates trust. He imitates obedience. He imitates submission. He imitates wisdom. He imitates law. He imitates faith. He imitates humility. He imitates truth. He imitates love. And he sells it to those who are taken in by his false advertisements at the costly price of their eternity.

Why are they so easily taken in by this master manipulator? Because they refuse to pay the price of the real or original merchandise. There is an old adage which goes, "You get what you pay for" and not one bit more. You can't get a Mercedes for the price of a Volkswagen. And you can't get a plane for the price of car. Nor can you get a yacht for the cost of a canoe. If you want a Mercedes, a plane or a yacht you've got to be able to make the financial investment required of you to take ownership of those assets. Saints, if you want to be a real prayer warrior, preacher, teacher, apostle, prophet or just child of God, then you've got to be willing to pay the full price. There is no such thing a discounted prayer warrior or a marked down evangelist or an anointing you can get on sale. THERE IS A PRICE TO BE PAID FOR THE GLORY OF GOD TO OPERATE IN YOUR LIFE!!!!!

In the natural we are able to distinguish between the real and the fake because we KNOW that we are going shopping for the FAKE. But in the spirit realm, we shop for, long for, hope for, pray for, petition for and desire the real, but we often take possession of the imitation. Why? Because we have not yet paid the price to develop a discerning Spirit.

Just know that every prophet is not of God. Every preacher is not sent by God. Every worshipper does not do so in spirit and in truth. Every praise is not genuine. And every pastor is not a God-sent shepherd! There are fakes in every aspect of existence. That is Satan's plan—to thoroughly deceive God's own elect and for the purpose of pulling them away from TRUTH via his wiles and plots of deception.

It is only when you know TRUTH, that you can hold it up against the imposter known as a lie and not be deceived. Your degrees cannot do this for you. Your titles cannot do this for you. Your positions cannot do this for you. Your memberships cannot do this for you. Your attending various conventions cannot do this for you. It is only through our knowledge of and intimate relationship with THE TRUTH that this can be done. There is no other way.

Often times, depending on how much you are willing to pay, the imitations look so much like the real thing that if you put them on a counter next to each other, only the most trained and expert eye can differentiate between them. Could this be why Jesus told us to let the wheat (real saints) and the tariff (fake saints) grow together, and when HE comes HE will divide them? Is it because the fakes so closely resemble the original that if WE tried to distinguish between them we could make crucial mistakes? But didn't just say that if our relationship were strong enough in Christ that we would be able to make the distinction? No. Not the distinction to separate others. Only the distinction to separate YOURSELF. He would not have us ignorant concerning the wiles (tricks, fakes, imitations) or the adversary.

Spiritual replicas are very exacting and strongly resemble their original counterparts. So much so that Jesus taught us that IN THAT DAY there will be much gnashing of teeth and many saying to Him, did we not preach, teach and cast out demons in your name. YET, he said, He will say unto them, depart from me you worker of iniquity. **I NEVER KNEW YOU**.

That's powerful! He didn't say I once knew (intimate as in a close and true relationship) you, but you backslid or you failed to endure unto the end. NO!! He said you were one of those who NEVER PAID THE FULL AND NECESSARY PRICE TO GET TO KNOW AND BECOME ONE OF MINE!! Yes you went to theology school; and yes, you pastured a church; and yes you lead praise and worship and yes you laid hands on the sick, but guess what you worker of iniquity? I NEVER KNEW YOU.

Of course the question will follow, if I am a worker of iniquity how then could I have done these things? And I'm sure Jesus will say "Because you did them in my name. And even though YOU were a fake, the power in my name is still REAL AND ORIGINAL! (Which is why at the sound of HIS name EVERY KNEE SHALL BOW AND EVERY TONGUE SHALL CONFESS!!!)

How cleaver is Satan? So cleaver that he is capable of using individuals who have no desire to be or knowledge that they are being used by him. That's how deceptive he is. The Bible says he is so deceptive that if these last days were not cut short that even the very elect of God would be deceived!

Listen. If you want a mansion, you can't bargain the payments down to that of apartment rent. If you want a diamond, you can't go shopping at the fake costume jewelry shop. If you want Rolls Royce, then stay off the used Chevrolet lot. Likewise if you want to be a REAL prayer warrior, you've got to study, pray, sacrifice, commune, fast, and vow to enter into a more intimate relationship with TRUTH. If you want to be a true praise and worshipper, preacher, teacher, apostle, prophet, evangelist, teacher or saint, the same holds true. "Wash them with truth of Lord. THY WORD IS TRUTH."

Only the TRUTH can lead us, guide us and protect us from the wiles of the great deceiver and father of all lies. Only the TRUTH can alert us to the wiles and steer us away from the traps and entrapments of the adversary. But will do this only to the extent of your personal INVESTMENT in Him.

God is free (to all men), but He's not cheap. A REAL relationship with God costs! He's not on discount. He is not discontinued. He isn't going out of business. And he is not a previous model. There is but one God. He was. He is. And He forever shall be. I would, and humbly do, encourage you to take the time to invest in Him and to pay the full price of the cost of quality relationship with Him. Just as Jesus paid the full cost of our salvation, despite the cost, we, likewise should pay the full cost of a REAL RELATIONSHIP WITH OUR LORD AND SAVIOR.

The choice is yours. You can hang on to your basement bargain relationships or dig deeper into your spiritual accounts and PAY THE FULL COST OF A QUALITY REALATIONSHIP WITH THE ONE AND ONLY QUALITY GOD. But whatever your decision is, I truly hope our Lord and Savior will never say to you "Depart from me you worker of iniquity. (You bargain hunter!) I never knew you.) After all, what does it profit a man to gain the whole world yet lose his bargain hunting soul? Think about it.

Know the truth (not a marked down replica) and the truth will make you free.

Blessings.

Thanksgiving is not a seasonal experience, it is a daily result of our gratitude to God for all He has done and is doing in our lives.

FIND SOMETHING NEW TO THANK GOD FOR EVERY SINGLE DAY

Thanksgiving is upon us. But this Thanksgiving day, what things will flood your being and press their way out of the dusty storage of your memory bank and into your present moment as being worthy of you giving thanks for them? Will it be the day God saved (rescued, redeemed, reclaimed) you? Or will it be the day Immanuel donned a covering of flesh and chose to dwell among men? Perhaps your thanksgiving will center itself on the victory of the cross and all it represents and did for humanity. Or maybe even you will be humbled as you reflect upon the power of the resurrection. Maybe your thanksgiving will be centered on the reality of the ascension, the upper room experience, the promises of the Master, the hope of eternal deliverance, or perhaps even upon the certainty of the return of our almighty savior to harvest us, His people, as the sanctified grains of His holy fields. Perhaps someone's thanksgiving will abound plentifully upon reflecting on how God miraculously touched and held their body, while another's thanksgiving might come forth as a mighty stream when they reflect on how the provisions of the almighty found their way into their life at just the right and crucial moment. Someone else's joy of thanksgiving may be ignited with just a cursory reflection of where God has brought them from and where he has brought them to. And on and on the inexhaustible list of reasons for thanksgiving grows.

But if you're not saved and if you do not know the glory and goodness of God, for what then do you have to give thanks? That too is easily answered. By virtue of the fact that you "are," (meaning that you exist, live breath, and move) is reason enough to give thanks. Inasmuch as you didn't or couldn't bring yourself into existence by yourself, of your own will or by your own power means that a higher more perfect power and will summoned, ordained, prepared, purposed and commissioned your very presence here. Likewise, this "source" being fully knowledgeable of all things, knew you're your total plight, plan and purpose and fully equipped you to overcome every single obstacle, challenge and destructive device of evil that you would ever encounter. And for that thanks should be offered up. Because you can see the beauty of the Creator's handiwork and are not without sight, you have something that is thanks worthy. Because you can open up your mouth and send forth praises and thanks yourself and are not neither deaf or dumb, you have reasons worthy of thanks giving. Because of your functioning mind, working body parts and your life itself, you have much to be thankful for.

The very fact that God would not allow you to be born in a third world country, be subject to the dictatorship of an atheistic government or permit the devil to claim your life before you have had many opportunities to chose Him as your lord and savior are all reasons why you ought to thank him today. That God has always turned his face to us, even when we chose to turn our backs to him (for sin) is reason to give thanks today. When we reflect on the number of instances wherein our lives could have been snuffed out, but God divinely intervened and told death to move elsewhere because you were protected by him is worthy of thanks. Many of us will throw away more food between Thanksgiving, Christmas and New Years than some families will have to eat the entire year is just one more reason to say Lord, I thank You. When we think back and remember that many of us don't even wear the same clothes this year that we did last year (mostly out of vanity) and consider that there are people who don't have houses, closets or seasonal selections of clothes in them, how blessed we are! Why would we not say God, I give You thanks? Children will return home from college and generate many fond smiles and much laughter as they will gaily recall their life changing college experiences. Normal? Not if You live in a country where women cannot attend school at all and the average level of education for the males is around third grade. God, we thank You.

Father, for all that You have been doing for us every second of our existence, even when we didn't know or acknowledge it, we thank You today. We thank You for Your love, Your kindness, Your forgiveness, Your mercy, Your grace, Your presence, Your virtue, Your peace, Your provisions, Your healing, Your fellowship, Your promises, Your faithfulness and the certainty of the veracity of every one of Your words. How deficient we are in our ability to sufficiently thank You. For how can a single tongue thank You for the blessings You began bestowing upon us before the foundation of the world? Thank You for Your grace that is greater than sufficient in all cases. Thank You for Your forgiveness every time I mess up. Thank You for Your love that would not allow You to cast me from Your presence. Thank You for calling, choosing, equipping, ordaining and sending me forth. Thank You for every provision You have lavished upon my life. Thank You for Your Spirit of Truth and Your son, Jesus Christ, who disrobed himself of His God-likeness (divinity) and took on my sin that I might have the ability and the right to be called Your child. Thank You for every stripe that Jesus humbled himself and took on my behalf that I would not have to be subject to it myself. Thank You for His persecution that I might not have to suffer it. Thank You for His visit into the pit that I might have the right to sit in heavenly places with You and Him. Thank You for His words of truth, power and wisdom for without them, I could never be washed, claimed, redeemed, or adopted into Your royal family. Thank You for the obedience of Jesus, my savior, for without His obedience there would be no passageway from the kingdom of sin to the kingdom of glory. If I didn't say it when I rose this morning, let me say it now . . . THANK YOU GOD!! If I didn't say it when I spoke to my wife, son, daughter, mother, brothers or sisters, nieces or nephews today, let me shout it from the mountain top of my heart right now . . . THANK YOU GOD. If I didn't say it when You woke me up yesterday, if I didn't say it when You allowed me to matriculate through various schools, if I didn't say it when You healed me, if I didn't say it when You blessed me, if I didn't say it when You saved me, if I didn't say it when You kept me, if I didn't say it when You protected me, if I didn't say it when You empowered me, if I didn't say it when You forgave me, if I didn't say it when You enlightened me . . . then let me say it now . . . THANK YOU GOD. And if I did say it in all of those and on every other occasion, You are worthy of a repeated praise and thanks so let me say it again and again and again . . . LORD I THANK YOU! LORD I THANK YOU! LORD I THANK YOU! LORD I THANK YOU! IN JESUS NAME I THANK YOU.

Blessings.

For they that are after the flesh do mind the things of the flesh; but they that are after the Spirit the things of the Spirit. For to be carnally minded is death; but to be spiritually minded is life and peace. Because the carnal mind is enmity against God: for it is not subject to the law of God, neither indeed can be. So then they that are in the flesh cannot please God. But ye are not in the flesh, but in the Spirit, if so be that the Spirit of God dwell in you. Now if any man have not the Spirit of Christ, he is none of His.

Some Times Since Doesn't Make Sense

I have found that so many would-be Christians refuse to follow and believe Christ because, they say, when I look at Jesus, there's a lot of stuff that just doesn't make sense. It doesn't make sense that a man could have walked on water. And it doesn't make sense that He could heal people just by speaking or touching them, or even them touching Him. It doesn't make sense that He would forgive those who were crucifying Him. And it sure doesn't make sense that He could cause the wind and the rain to peace be still, a fig tree to dry up at the root, a blind man to rub spit and dirt over his blind eyes and receive sight, or for a dead man to return to life without Him even going into the tomb and praying over him. When I look at all of these things, they say, and consider that to compound this He was even born of a virgin and his birth was prophesied hundreds and hundreds of years before he came onto the scene. To me, these people confess, it doesn't make sense. And to them I confess, they are 100% correct. Very little about Jesus makes sense, but everything about Jesus makes FAITH. And that is what God wants us to have in order to please Him.

To these people I often say you're confused because you're operating in the wrong "sense". The sense in which they are operating is that of the carnal mind, which is enmity toward God and the things of God and cannot perceive or receive the things of the Spirit. For it was given unto us as a guide for the natural or physical realm, but not as a connector to the Spiritual realm. Within each of us is another "device" given to all men for that purpose. It is called the spirit of man. And when the Spirit of God comes to dwell in the spirit of man, the Holy Spirit "quickens" (or makes alive) the spirit of man which was previously dead to God and His ways ("For to be carnally minded is death; but to be spiritually minded is life and peace. Because the carnal mind is enmity against God: for it is not subject to the law of God, neither indeed can be. So then they that are in the flesh cannot please God. But ye are not in the flesh, but in the Spirit, if so be that the Spirit of God dwell in you.") That is why we were slaves to our sinful nature. Our spirits had no connection to the Father of Light and Good. And so we obeyed (with joy) our then-master and sinned with bountiful pleasure and expectation. But now we are no longer slaves to sin but slaves to righteousness and we no longer yield our instruments to the conduct of sin.

Therefore, I know that many of the acts and miracles of Christ do not make sense to many people. It is yet a mystery to them because they are yet to say as Mary did, "Be it unto me according to thy Word." Once we release ourselves from the "sense" notation of Christ, we will be able to arrive at the "since" reality of Him. I confess much of it will not make sense until you allow Him to convert your skepticism into confidence and your ignorance into wisdom. Once this transformation takes place, you will never again say "sense" when it comes to the things of the Kingdom of God. Instead, you will always find yourself saying "since".

In other words, how does a man spit on dirt and rub it across the eyes of a blind man and restore sight? I don't know and I admit it doesn't make sense intellectually, medically or scientifically, but SINCE He did it, I know that He can use anything He wishes to perform a miracle.

How does He stand outside of a tomb and call a decaying, dead man back to life? I don't know and surely it doesn't make "sense," but SINCE He did it I know that He can work a miracle in anybody's life without ever laying a hand on their physical body. How does a woman who has had a severe illness for many years and has seen all of the best doctors simply touch the hem of his garment and be made whole? I can't explain it in any way that would make "sense," but SINCE it happened, I'll just compelled that much more to know that if I can touch but the hem of His garment, I too shall be made whole.

How could Jesus walk on water? Feed a multitude and have leftovers when He started with no enough? How can He command the winds and the rains to obey Him? How does He speak to demons and they obey? How does the wisdom of a 12 year old, unschooled carpenter's son stump the knowledge of the best Jewish teachers of His day? Does this make sense to you? Of course not. And it was never given to us that it might make sense. It was given to us that it might make FAITH and relationship. Our words should be "SINCE YOU DID IT" what wise choice do I have but to trust You? SINCE history, as well as the Bible, has recorded Your birth and life and miracles and crucifixion and resurrection and ascension, why would I not believe and trust in You? Did Buddha do these things? Did Confucius do them? Did Elijah Muhammad do them? Is there another one who EVER left glory and descended into human flesh to redeem mankind? Has there been another resurrection since Yours? Is there another Advocate or Mediator between Mortality and immortality, between the Creator and the created? Is there another name whereby we can be saved or is there another once whom the angels delivered His name and the heavens revealed His coming? Of course not. But SINCE You and You alone fit this bill, how can I not call you my Lord?

If we wait for God to make sense to us, we'll die in our skepticism. At some point we have to simply choose by faith, believe by faith, live by faith and come into the wisdom and understanding of the Greater One by faith.

Since He's a known miracle worker; and since He's a demonstrated redeemer; and since He's a documented healer; and since He's commanded all things-be they powers, principalities, rulers of the darkness, or whatever—and they have obeyed Him;

and since He is the only source with a traceable history back to pre-creation days; and since all power and authority has been given unto Him by the Father, why not stop trying to make "sense" of him and just say Father SINCE . . . .

Trust me, you will never arrive at the "since" of God until you choose to get passed the "sense" of man.

Blessings.

When a person's ways are pleasing to the LORD, He makes even his enemies to be at peace with him.

For am I now seeking the approval of man, or of God? Or am I trying to please man? If I were still trying to please man, I would not be a servant of Christ.

But just as we have been approved by God to be entrusted with the gospel, so we speak, not to please man, but to please God who tests our hearts.

I have been crucified with Christ. It is no longer I who live, but Christ who lives in me. And the life I now live in the flesh I live by faith in the Son of God, who loved me and gave himself for me.

Whatever you do, work heartily, as for the Lord and not for men . . .

The fear of man lays a snare, but whoever trusts in the Lord is safe.

Just Do You

Have you ever been around folks who are one way on Monday, another way on Tuesday and altogether different on Wednesday? Have you been around folks who are one way around Christians, another way around sinners, another way around professional colleagues and yet another way in the community? Isn't it confusing? Isn't it perplexing? Doesn't it make you want to ask them "Just who the heck are you and what the heck are you all about? Because truly it's hard for me to tell! I can't tell because one minute you're hot; the next minute you're cold; the next minute you're warm; the next minute you're boiling, and the following minute you're freezing. WHO ARE YOU? Are you a saint or are you a sinner? Are you operating in the kingdom of light or in the kingdom of darkness? Are you a holy ambassador or are you of your father the devil, who is the author of all lives since the beginning?"

It's confusing not just to saints and sisters and brothers in Christ, but it's even more confusing to those you are out of Christ, out of the kingdom, and out of the righteousness of God. They are even more confused by your myriad vacillations. So much so that many will not accept the reality and veracity of this way of life because Christians are too busy being identified and associated with the things and ways of the world. ("Love not the word or the things in the world.") Politics is now shaping the focus of

Christian hope. Celebrities (mere mortal human beings) are now becoming the idols of believers. Our trust is now more in legislation than in the Word. Our walk is now based more on what the prognosticators are predicting than what the Word of God has promised. Our deliverance and salvation are now based more on the doctrines of institutions than they are faith based. Our spiritual leaders are now being trained and ordained more so by universities than are being ordained, predestined and sent by God.

Why has all of this come to be? Because Christians have become too chameleon-like to retain and to reflect the power, the grace and the anointing of God in the earth realm. What I mean by this is that Christians are trying too desperately to be politically, socially, intellectually, or professionally correct in all that do and say about God our Father. Very few of us seem to want to speak in tongues anymore because our intellect tells us that such "foolishness" is unnecessary and is not required by today's men and women of God. And so, regardless of what the Word of God says, (tongues . . .) we consciously make a decision to fit in with the common and accepted thinking of those who are not truly of us. Believers are retreating from their duties of laying hands on the sick because some medical and legal minds have opposed their rights to do so. Evangelists have grown silent because they have become too tied up with other worldly issues and concerns to take the Word of God into every highway and byway and compel men to come to Christ. Those whom God has called have become too societally perfected, necessary and conscious to do the single most important thing any saved person can do, that is to carry out his divine mission while here in the earth realm.

But today I just want to challenge every reader of this word to immediately start—ON PURPOSE—doing one simple thing and to continue to do it for the rest of their life. If you are reading this, I want you to decree this day, that henceforth, now and forever more that you will <u>JUST DO YOU!</u>

What does it mean to just do you? It means that once and for all, you will stop caring about what folks may say about you and you will start caring more about what God has decreed about you. You will stop acting out of people's expectation of you and start to act our God's expectations. You will not be ashamed to lift up your hands, send up your prayerful voice, shout, run, jump, testify, minister, pray, or to do any and all of the things God has ordained and released into you to do for His glory and in His service and honor while you are in this realm. For once in your life you will honor the power, the grace, the blessing and the assignment of God upon your life and you will not vacate, abandon, ignore or subordinate them to the wishes, understanding, expectations, or words of anyone else (regardless of who they may be, what they may say or what it may cost you). From this day forward you will take authority over your own spiritual relationship, destiny and manifestation by JUST DOING YOU.

The weak need to stand and say, I will no longer operate out of the spirit of intimidation, fear and weakness. For this is not the spirit which comes from my Father dwells in me. I am strong. I am a warrior. I am a victor. In all of these things I am more than a conqueror. And from this day forward I will no longer just KNOW who I am, but now since I know it, I'll walk it out. In other words, from this day forward I'm going to JUST DO ME.

The songsters will no longer walk about humming their sprit-felt praises, but will sing them aloud as God has placed them in their spirits. They will make a joyful noise unto the Lord. They will glorify Him in song and praise. They will lift up their voices to praise God in their homes, on their jobs, in their cars, in the places of sickness, on the streets, in every stressful situation and in the services of God. Their voices will serve as divine trumpets for humanity and will set ablaze something new and powerful in the atmosphere. Their voices will, like an angelic clarion call welcoming in the power, the peace and the presence of God as God Himself will anoint their vocal cords to address the very issues, infirmities and situations of those in their presence. But this they can do only if they make the empowering commitment to just "DO ME".

Ministers, pastors, preachers, apostles, and teachers will speak words of truth, wisdom, power, understanding, healing, enlightenment and encouragement that will change the course of the hearers' destiny and eternity. They will cast out demons, lay hands on the sick and they will recover, speak with new tongues, teach men to obey the laws and statues of God the Father, and serve as Holy instruments of covering and prayerful protection over those over whom God has placed them as watchmen. But this none of them can do until they vow the vow of spiritual commitment to "JUST DO ME".

Musicians and dancers will play and dance as unto the Lord and say not a word, yet the anointing and power of God shall go forth and greatly empower their every note and movement, that as ears hear and eyes see, the spirit will receive and will be transformed, set free, and revived into a new life which is abundant only in Christ. But this they can do only after each has truly covenant with God to "Just Do Me".

Far too long now, we've allowed tradition, manmade doctrine, dogma, and natural laws and rules to dictate what it would take for us to be all that God would have us to be. But the Word of God reminds us to work out our own soul salvation by fear and trembling. One songstress put it this way, "You don't know the cost of the oil in my alabaster box." In other words, you don't know why I praise the way I do, or why I pray as hard as I do, or why I shout so much as I do or even why I cry pools of tears when I come into the presence of God. You don't know. You don't know because you weren't there when God healed someone from cancer. And you weren't there when without a pill or a surgeon's knife, He meticulously removed a deadly virus from somebody's body. You don't know because you were not the prostitute on the street or gang banger on the corner. You don't know. You don't know how He brought someone out of prison and someone else through the consequences of rape. You don't know the cost of their praise. You don't know the cost (conditions and situations that God has brought someone through) of the oil (praise) in their alabaster box (heart/spirit).

But, since they do, and since God has done all of these abundantly great miracles in their lives, should they not give Him the real level of praise and worship He is due? I submit, they never can unless they decide for themselves that henceforth, I'm just going to JUST DO ME.

Fathers, do you. Be the man unto whom your family looks for guidance, love and spiritual and natural support. Mothers, do you. Be that Proverbs 31 woman of virtue. Children, do you. Obey your mothers and your fathers for this is right with the Lord who promises to bless your children as a result.

If you are a true believer, I urge you to do you and to not shrink back from the guidance and leading of the Holy Spirit. Sinners are doing themselves and their thing. They are bold, brash, intentional and unapologetic. And if they can adopt such an attitude while serving an inferior, defeated foe, how much more bold and purposeful should we, the children of the Most High, be with our praise and about our image?

Do you. Walk by faith and not by sight and do you. Rejoice, I say again, rejoice, and do you. Forget those things are behind you and press forward toward the mark of the higher calling in Christ Jesus and do you. Be ye emulators of Christ Jesus and do you. Never can your fullness be recognized, realized or materialized as long as you fail to fully do you.

In the name of Jesus, our Christ, I encourage you brothers and sisters, please, by the authority, grace, power and purpose of God upon your life . . . regardless of what else is going on around you . . . to have the courage and the conviction to <u>JUST DO YOU.</u>

> There comes a time in every man's education,
> when he arrives at the conviction that envy is
> ignorance and imitation is suicide . . . that he must
> take himself, for better or for worse, as his own
> portion in life . . . And though the wide universe
> is full of good, no kernel of nourishing corn will come
> his way except through the toil he bestows upon that
> plot of land which is given unto him to till. The power
> which resides in him is new in nature and no one
> knows what it is he can do, neither does he until he has tried.
> (Ralph W. Emerson, Self Reliance)

Blessings.

I am the way, the truth, and the life. No one comes to the Father except through Me

His Word Is My Truth

Realizing that God cannot lie and that His word will not return unto Him void is a powerful revelation. To lie is to give forth a false statement or impression. It is to deceive or to distort. It is to promulgate disinformation for the purpose of manipulation or misguiding. But the Word of God CANNOT do any of these of any other such negative thing because the Word of God is pure, holy, inerrant, accurate truth. Therefore, whatever God has spoken into your spirit about you, or promised you, or divinely commissioned you to do or ordained you to be, it is so. Are you not a prophet simply because you're not prophesying? I contend that's not the case at all. Conversely, I believe that you are a prophet, however, you are operating contrary to your divine appointment, orders, commission, power, purpose and abilities. Suppose your natural father said to you that he was placing $10 million in a trust for you for your personal use once you become 21 years old. However, once you became 21 you did not see your father anymore and so you thought that he'd not kept his word and had abandoned you. Nonetheless, he had done exactly as he had promised. He actually placed the funds in an account with only your name on it as the access code. Subsequently you fell upon hard times and found yourself living on the streets, under bridges and in dilapidated houses with the downtrodden of society. My question is, are you an indigent and poor person or are you a rich person who has not accessed the promised left to you by your father? Did your father lie or did you fail to believe his word, receive it and go and access your account of wealth?

This is the way we do God. He has faithfully promised us blessings, authority, gifts, power and dominion. He has assured us that He is our provider and sustainer. He has told us that He is our strong tower and He has given us His peace. And then He has topped it off by letting us know that all of the promises of God are YES (it is done) and AMEN (now may the words of my mouth be made manifest in my life).

God never lies to us. Whatever He says about us IS. He ordained Jeremiah a prophet unto the nations while He was yet in the womb. Paul said He had been chosen to preach the gospel before he was separated from his mother's womb. Did they have to do these things? They could have resisted. They could have not believed. They could have opposed. But they didn't. They believed the word of God as absolute truth. They received it as a promise from the Almighty One. And they applied it to their lives and conducted themselves according to their callings each day. As a result, the Word of God, which was spoken about, over and into them took root in their spirits, transformed their minds and crucified their flesh and carnal desires in order that that Word would be realized and manifested through their earthly vessels in this realm unto the glory of God.

So what has God been saying about and to you? Whatever God has spoken into your spirit man about you, is absolute truth. It is void of deception, manipulation, falsehood or trickery. It is truth in its purest and most accurate form. Even if you don't receive it as truth, it is still undistorted and uncompromised truth.

Why are you fearful and embarrassed to be what God has promised you? His word does not lie neither does it return unto Him void. Rather, His word simply enlightens us of God's plans for and expectations of us.

Stop resisting. Stop trying to control it. You were designed by a master creator who gave you purpose, power and destiny at the time He created you. Why not honor your calling? Why not honor God? Why not, as the Army would say it, "Be all that you can be?"

The Word of God is true and does not lie. It goes forth to make known the will of the Father unto His children and does not return unto Him void. Listen closely to God's unique voice in your spirit and receive it as His truth about you.

Blessings.

I'm Going Into Battle; I
Need a Few Good Men

No man will be able to stand before you all the days of your life. As I was with Moses, so I will be with you. I will not fail you nor forsake you. "Be strong and courageous; for you shall cause this people to inherit the land which I swore to their fathers to give them. Only be strong and very courageous, to observe to do according to all the law, which Moses my servant commanded you. Don't turn from it to the right hand or to the left, that you may have good success wherever you go. This book of the laws (Bible) shall not depart out of your mouth, but you shall meditate on it day and night, that you may observe to do according to all that is written therein: for then you shall make your way prosperous, and then you shall have good success." (Joshua 1:5-8)

Finally, my brethren, be strong in the Lord and in the power of his might. Put on the whole armor of God, that ye may be able to stand against the wiles of the devil. For we wrestle not against flesh and blood, but against principalities, against powers, against the rulers of the darkness of this world, against spiritual wickedness in high places. Wherefore take unto you the whole armor of God, that ye may be able to withstand in the evil day, and having done all, to stand. Stand therefore, having your loins girt about with truth, and having on the breastplate of righteousness; And your feet shod with the preparation of the gospel of peace; Above all, taking the shield of faith, wherewith ye shall be able to quench all the fiery darts of the wicked. And take the helmet of salvation, and the sword of the Spirit, which is the word of God: praying always with all prayer and supplication in the Sprit, and watching thereunto with all perseverance and supplication for all saints (Eph. 6: 10-19).

For though we walk in the flesh, we do not war after the flesh: (For the weapons of our warfare are not carnal, but mighty through God to the pulling down of strong holds, Casting down imaginations, and every high thing that exalteth itself against the knowledge of God, and bringing into captivity every thought to the obedience of Christ; And having in a readiness to revenge all disobedience, when your obedience is fulfilled. (2 Cor 10:4-6)

The Bible teaches us to resist or oppose (with the Word and our faith) the devil and he will flee. But the Bible never told us that once he leaves that he would STAY gone. Conversely, this unwelcomed guest never stays away long enough. Instead he goes out and rounds up a few more of his boys and returns strengthened and reinforced. This time he means business. His aim is to destroy you from the inside out. His strategy is to attack you in every area of your being that has been strengthened to repel his demonic attacks and evil strategy. His purpose is to disrupt, corrupt, intimidate, deceive, torture and mislead. His goal is to personally welcome you to your eternal home. No matter how dressed up, how convincing, how persuasive and logical, how enticing, how articulate or how informed he may impress you as being, the one thing you must remember is that he is the adversary and he opposes all that is good in you, for you and that can come out of you. His resume is short: The father of all lies and a master deceiver. His intent too can be summed up in a single sentence: He comes but for to kill, steal and destroy.

This enemy has infiltrated our territory long enough! And today, even if I have to go alone, I'm taking this boy his eviction notice. And I am not going to simply give the notice to him either, but this day I am taking the Word of God, my authority from heaven and God's omnipotent power as I will not email, snail mail or facebook this notice to him. Rather, I am prepared to walk up, face-to-face, with this defeated foe and to hand him a Holy Ghost notice of eviction to let him know that he was only an illegal spiritual squatter from day one. For every territory(heart) that he has sought to take, divert, possess or deceive was never his from the beginning—but simply lost souls who have been duked and deceived by his lying, cunning, and sly ways.

But thanks be to God, the Father has prepared me specifically and meticulously for just such warfare. I, like Joshua, am told in my spirit to "Be strong and courageous; for you shall cause this people to inherit the land which I swore to their fathers to give them. Only be strong and very courageous, to observe to do according to all the law, which Moses my servant commanded you. Don't turn from it to the right hand or to the left, that you may have good success wherever you go. This book of the laws (Bible) shall not depart out of your mouth, but you shall meditate on it day and night, that you may observe to do according to all that is written therein: for then you shall make your way prosperous, and then you shall have good success."

The battle is not so much about me as it is about others. For just as God told Joshua his strength and courage would cause [this] people to inherit the land which I swore to their father to give them, I too know that when I take my rightful place in this fight, my strength and courage will bring into fruitful and bountiful manifestation, the myriad of promises that have been spoken and reserved for others.

But, too, I know that iron (righteous men) sharpeneth (strengthen, undergird, counsel and support) iron (other righteous men). This is why I am searching for a few good men. A few good men who will stand on the Word of God no matter the challenge and opposition; a few good men who no matter what happens stand on the promise from the Father that in all these things we are more than conquerors. I'm looking for a few good men who can live and operate by the Kingdom's Code of Conduct and Ethics. A few good men who don't mind lifting up holy hands and giving God the glory. I'm looking for a few good men who do not love the world or the things in the world. I'm looking for a few good men who will observe to do all that God has commanded and commands of them. I'm looking for a few good men who won't allow any member of their bodies to be used to promote sin in any way. I'm looking for a few good men who are not ashamed of the Gospel of Jesus Christ. I'm looking for a few good men who know that God has not given unto us the spirit of fear, but of love and a sound mind. I'm looking for a few good men who will have no other God before Yahweh. I'm looking for a few good men who walk by faith and not by sight. I'm looking for a few good men who love and will serve the Father unto death.

In other words, I need a few good men who will sign up for a DIP mission. A DIP mission is a Die In Place mission. It's a dangerous mission into which, when you go, it is known that the statistical likelihood of your surviving is far less than the likelihood of your demise. Yet, you are so devoted to the mission that you forget about the dangers and the sacrifices, and instead you simply focus on the benefits of the mission. This is what Peter did. This is what Stephen did. This is what Jesus did.

But if you're afraid, fearful, double minded, without firm conviction and weak in faith, then this is not the place or fight for you. In this battle, there are no timeouts, coffee breaks, holidays or vacations. This is spiritual trench warfare. It's you and the enemies of hell coming face to face, repeated and often. It's you taking and immediately obeying the orders of your Heavenly Commander in Chief. It's you letting go of all that He may become your all. It's you refusing to abandon your Holy post until you have been properly relieved. It's you reporting for duty properly attired every day (The Armor of God) and thoroughly knowing and obeying your general orders (the Bible). It's you being in spiritual condition that will allow you to pray long prayers, battle with strongholds and praise without end.

Sometimes you're hungry (fasting) and sometimes you're in the foxhole all alone (private time with the Master). But these are the things that teach us how to fight as warriors! There is territory to be re-taken and blessings to be loosed. There are healings to be manifested and blessings to be received. There are demons to be cast out and grace to be activated. This is not a one man job, but I'll go in alone if that is what must be. I prefer to be sharpened by my brothers in Christ as I sharpen my brothers, but this is an all volunteer mission. You choose this mission. It doesn't choose you.

I cannot stand back and see hell's attacks and sicknesses and destructions continue to work in the lives of God's elect. This has to STOP and now! One believer can put 1000 demons to flight. Two can put 10,000 to flight. So how much demonic havoc can one hundred or one thousand saved men undo?

The kingdom suffereth violence but the violent TAKE IT BY FORCE. The devil does not relinquish territory without a fight—even if it's your divinely legal territory. Are you violent for Christ? Are you really a soldier of the cross? Or do you love your own life more than you do the needs of the Kingdom? If your answer is no, then sign up for battle!

Blessings.

HE WATCHES OVER HIS WORD
TO PERFORM IT. DO YOU?

What is our word worth to God? More personally, what is my word worth in the eyes and to the heart of God? Can God place as much confidence in my word as I can in His? Can He trust me to keep and faithfully abide by and to fulfill my every word as I can Him to do the same for His? I am saved by faith. Meaning I trust that my salvation is real and accomplished simply by the faith that I have placed in the God's word. I am delivered and kept by the power of God's word and my unyielding faith from the sin nature by which and into which I was originally conceived. I trust and place my entire eternity in God's hand because I sincerely trust and believe in his every word. It's rewarding, refreshing and re-assuring to know that I can in fact trust God, believe God and rely on Him to always do just what His word has promised. What a testimony to His character, to His integrity, to His veracity, to His faithfulness and to His stewardship over His own word. No one else comes to mind or measures up to the level of trust that I place in Him and His word. He is all that He has said He will be in, to, over, through, around and for me. He does everything that His word promises He would. He delivers on His every pledge and makes manifest His every utterance. He is steadfast, passionate and unwavering when it comes to holding fast to his forever settled word. Truly God is exactly what and who He says He is and He does nothing less than everything that He promises in His word.

However, the question is not is God true to His word when it comes to us, but, rather, are we true to our word when it comes to Him. We are certain, based upon our experiences with Him, that we indeed can place our full trust, hope and confidence in God's every word. About that there is no doubt. But if God had to hang the future of heaven on our word, what would be heaven's outcome? Could God say about us, based upon our adherence to our word, what we are now able to say about Him based upon His adherence to His word? Could God count us faithful? Loyal? Trustworthy? Dedicated? Honest? Sincere? Without guile? Pure? Positive? Loving? Kind? Patient? Or just religiously talkative?

Would we promise God a given behavior when in the midst of difficulties and demonstrate a different behavior after He has delivered us? Will we speak boldly only among other Christians and timidly when among the vipers of a wayward generation? Could God actually count on us to do what we promised Him we would if He would just do (whatever) this one time? If we promise God we will speak His word if He would anoint us and place His word upon our tongue, would we do it if the individual to whom we are to speak is our agnostic boss? If we promise God that we will speak into the perishing souls of the sick and the dying, would we hold fast to our promise if the soul into which we are sent is that of a dying poor, homeless, unsaved, HIV victim or perhaps an obviously demon possessed person? If we promise God that we would lift up His Holy name in song and praise at all times, would we abandon our promise when the non-Christians begin to complain about our disturbing Christian activities? If we promise God that we are going to study His yoke destroying word, can God take us at our word or should He know to place an asterisk behind our promise and to take it with a grain of salt. (After all, He "knows our heart." Right? And therefore He already knows that the TV always comes before the kingdom.)

My point is that we trust God because we know we can rely on Him to remain faithful to His word. But if God were trying to get to know us based on our word, exactly what would He know about us? That we are easily discouraged? Fatigued? Angered? Frustrated? Intimidated? Made jealous? Spiteful? Rebellious? Insincere? Without holy stability? Lacking in dedication? Destitute of a true will to live out what we speak out? Void of spiritual intensity and integrity? Vacuous in our prayers? Vain in ourselves and selfish in our desires? What would He know about us if He had only the fruit of our lips to judge us by? Would our hearts be half as full as our mouths? Would our spirits be as committed as our outward behavior suggests? Would the true meditations of our heart be worthy of acceptance in His Holy and divine sight and presence?

God is inseparable from His word. The Bible says in the beginning was the word and the word was with God and the word was God and by Him (God's spoken word) was everything made that was made. The number one way we have come to know God is by way of His word and His faithfulness to it. How, then, do you think God has come to know you? And do you think that God takes our empty promises likely? Read Matthew 5:37 and see what Jesus teaches us about our words. Read Ecclesiastes 5:4-7 and see how God feels about our words. Numbers 30:2 makes it perfectly clear how God sees us and our word. Proverbs 19:1, Titus 2:7-8, Proverbs 12:22 and 25, Ephesians 4:24-25 and several other scriptures will bring in plain view how God sees and values our word offered to Him.

God holds us accountable for our words and He warns us to never make an offer or promise to Him then fail to keep it. He says it is better for us not to have ever made the promise than to renege on it. Does that not suggest to you that God takes very seriously the fruit of our lips and our every word offered up to Him? Maybe . . . just maybe . . . it's about time we did too.

Blessings.

For all the promises of God in Him are yea, and in Him AMEN, unto the glory of God by us.

Blessing and glory and wisdom and thanksgiving and honor and power and might be unto our God forever and ever. AMEN.

To the only wise God our Savior, be glory and majesty, dominion and power, both now and ever. AMEN.

And the God of peace shall bruise Satan under your feet shortly. The grace of our Lord Jesus Christ be with you. Blessed be the Lord God of Israel from everlasting to everlasting: and let all of the people say, AMEN.

In the natural, amen is just one word which means very little to many who often use it carelessly and without sincere conviction. The purpose of this teaching is to encourage individuals to agree with God's every word spoken over their lives many of which were spoken even before the foundation of the world but are still active and true today. To do this, all that is needed is for them to read the Word of God, believe it, receive it and seal their agreement with a simple amen said to God concerning His spoken declaration and promises over their lives.

God Has Spoken . . . So Why Won't You Say Amen?

I recently hard a beautiful song performed. The name of it was "Let the Church Say Amen". The lyrics were simple but powerful to those who were listening with their spiritual ears. The words merely said "Let the church say 'amen'. Let the church say 'amen'. God has spoken, so let the church say 'amen.'" As I sat under the spiritual anointing of the inspired message of the song, I began to not only love God more and more with the singing of every word, but deep down in my spirit I prayed that God would likewise allow someone else who was hearing these powerful words to receive the truth and the yoke destroying message that going forth in the form of a song. I began to pray that the obedience to the commands of the song's lyrics would be heeded and obeyed.

GOD HAS SPOKEN SO LET THE CHURCH SAY AMEN!!

The word amen simply acknowledges agreement with and acceptance of the spoken word, petition or testimony of another. Literally, the single word Amen means now may the spoken words of my mouth be made manifest in my life. We send up a petition (prayer) to the Throne of Glory then conclude it with amen because we want God to know that we, as David said, have believed, therefore we have spoken (prayed) it. And, of course, His Word of Promise teaches us that we can have whatsoever thing we ask when we pray believing. We end the prayer with amen because we now tell God that it is with these words that I set my heart, faith and spirit in agreement and fully expect to see their manifestation in my life. We say amen when there is a soul stirring message coming forth from a vessel of God because we agree with what we are hearing. When our friends make comments with which we really agree and believe are true, we usually chime in with an "amen sister!" or "amen brother!" What we are really saying by our use of the word amen is that I accept, believe and receive what you are saying as truth.

GOD HAS SPOKEN . . .

Now that God has spoken certain promises over, into and for us, why is it that we have such a hard time saying amen to Him whom we know is the Spirit of Truth as well as ". . . the way, the TRUTH and the life"? Why do we continue to tell people that we are just sinners saved by grace when God has spoken that if we are in Christ old things are passed away and all things are new? In other words we are now new creations. Why are we debating it as opposed to simply saying AMEN about it? Why do we keep accepting the report of the deceiver which tries to convince us that we are weaklings when God has told us that He has granted power from on high and spiritual authority unto all of His children to thread upon every evil power and serpent that we will ever encounter? Why do we keep returning to the vomit of a sinful way of life when God has told us that sin no longer has dominion, authority or power over us? Why do we keep believing that there are things in the spirit which we cannot achieve when God's own words teach us that nothing shall be impossible to those who believe? Why are believers still angry, distressed, anxious, and worried when God said to us let your heart be anxious for nothing and my peace I leave with you.

AMEN, GOD SIMPLY BECAUSE YOU HAVE DECREED IT AND I HAVE RECEIVED IT!!

Many believers have no idea just how much smoother, more peaceful, more impactful, more powerful, more fulfilled and more meaningful their lives would be if only they would simply say Amen, God. Amen to every promise He has decreed. Amen to every curse He has broken. Amen to every provision He provided. Amen to every miracle He has worked. Amen to every illness He has cured. Amen to every situation He has already set in you favor. Amen to every generational curse He has eliminated from our paths and out of our lives. Amen to every pray God has answered before you have even submitted it to Him. Amen to every evil spirit, power and dominion He has bound in your life and on your behalf. Amen to every blessing—known and unknown, petitioned and non-petitioned, seen and unseen, that He has already availed in your life despite your shortcomings. Amen to your gift of salvation. Amen to your anointing. Amen to the protection of your guardian angels who are encamped round about you and harken unto the voice of God whose thoughts toward you are good, pleasing and prosperous continually. Amen to your miracles. Amen to your peace, power, joy, praise, spiritual liberty and worship. Amen to your adoption into the royal family. Amen to your supernatural abilities and powers. Amen from the rising of the sun to the going down of the same. You, Father, have spoken it, I have believed, received and set my faith in agreement with it and today I boldly shout AMEN as a witness to Your faithful performance of Your every Holy, righteous and promised Word. Amen! And Amen!

DON'T FORGET TO SAY AMEN!!

You cannot love God and not agree with Him. You cannot obey God and not trust His word. You cannot be faithful to a word which you do not trust, believe, receive or act upon. Reading the Word of God is both good and necessary, but reading the Word alone is not enough. Quoting it is not enough. Sharing it with strangers is not enough. Sitting under it during Sunday morning services is not enough. While all of these things are good, necessary and required of each of us as a believer, it yet cannot be ignored or omitted that at some point in our Christian walk, if we are going to be elevated from glory to glory by the power and wisdom of God, it cannot or will not come until each of us personally and genuinely say Amen to what God has said about us in order for it to become manifested (made alive, real and tangible) in our lives.

Yes, whether it's said today, next week, next month or next year, at some point every believer MUST confess a genuine amen unto the honor, glory, power and faithfulness of God our Father. It is not a recommendation. It is not a good idea. It is not just a right thing to do. It is a spiritual imperative and a God-directed law. Until we bring our faith in line with what God has spoken about us and receive it in our spiritual man (with a genuine amen to God) we will only know what God has and desires for us, but we will never see it's full manifestation in our personal lives, ministries, marriage, health or endeavors.

It's not difficult and it's totally personal. If you want what God has for you start receiving it today by reviewing what He has said about, over, and for you and simply respond with Amen.

Blessings.

"God has spoken, let the church say amen."

A Pause for One Final Prayer

God, I thank you for having given me such a simplistic yet powerful word of confirmation of Your every Holy, empowering, soul saving, yoke destroy, burden lifting, spirit restoring salvation bringing, deliverance activating word You have provided as a spiritual safety net over every aspect of my life. Never do I have to lack because You have provided my every need out of Your boundless heavenly provisions. Never am I alone for You are the friend who sticks closer than any brother and will never leave me or forsake me. Never shall I be overtaken by the ploys of the evil one for You will not have me ignorant concerning the wiles of the deceiver. Never shall I operate in the spirit of fear for I now agree with Your word which teaches me that You have not given me the spirit of fear but of sound mind and love. God, I thank you for the liberty that You have released in my tongue to praise, my spirit to receive, my ears to hear and my eyes to see. Yes I will life up Holy hand everywhere I go for to render myself a living sacrifice unto Your glory which is but my reasonably duty. I am strong. I am protected. I am loved. I am worthy. I am powerful. I am cherished. I am righteous. I am sanctified. I am a child of the Kingdom of Light. No weapon that is formed against me shall prosper and the gates of hell cannot prevail against me. I cannot lose when I trust and obey You because greater is He (You) which is in me that he (the deceiver) that is in the world. I have world overcoming power and sin no longer has dominion and power over me. And while one thousand may fall at my left hand and ten thousand may fall at my right hand, evil shall not come neigh my dwelling, and this not because of my power or my might, but because of your supreme Spirit. I have your liberty, power, authority and permission to ask whatever heavenly and kingdom related thing that I may, and every time that I ask it in faith and do not waiver from my faith or ask amiss, surely I shall receive it. I not only expect miracles in my life from You, but I am a miracle working vessel in the earth realm for You. You are my Lord, my God, my Savior, my Father and my All. You are the source of all good things unto me and to You I humbly and readily give You this credit and honor. Bless me mightily God, not for me, but so that I may be a mighty blessing unto Your kingdom, the ministry of reconciliation and the ongoing battle of the spirits. You, God, are my power, my might and the Spirit which gives will, guidance and ability to my spirit. Let me never ever stray from the veracity of every letter of Your word. For it is to the extent that I know Your word that I know You. It is to the extent that I enact Your word that I can demonstrate You. And it only to the extent that I demonstrate You that I can receive manifestation of Your presence, anointing, grace and power at work in me and in my life. Yes, God, I will let my light so shine that men may see You in me and ask "What must I do to be saved?" I love You. I truly do. I believe You. I trust in You. I honor You. I glory in You. And I set all that I am in agreement with You by speaking this single word of agreement today—AMEN.

His Spirit and Life I Leave With You

For God is not unjust so as to overlook your work and the love that you have shown for His name in serving the saints, as you still do.

So then let us pursue what makes for peace and for mutual upbuilding . . .

Be kind to one another, tenderhearted, <u>forgiving one another</u>, as God in Christ forgave you.

Bearing with one another and, if one has a complaint against another, <u>forgiving each other</u>; as the Lord has forgiven you, so you also must forgive.

"Pay attention to yourselves! If your brother sins, rebuke him, and if he repents, <u>forgive him</u>, and if he sins against you seven times in the day, and turns to you seven times, saying, 'I repent,' <u>you must forgive him</u>."

"Judge not, and you will not be judged; condemn not, and you will not be condemned; <u>forgive, and you will be forgiven</u>.

Put on then, as God's chosen ones, holy and beloved, compassionate hearts, kindness, humility, meekness, and patience, bearing with one another and, if one has a complaint against another, <u>forgiving each other</u>; as the Lord has forgiven you, so you also must forgive.

And whenever you stand praying, forgive, if you have anything against anyone, so that your Father also who is in heaven may forgive you your trespasses.

Be angry and do not sin; do not let the sun go down on your anger . . .

To another he said, "Follow me." But he said, "Lord, let me first go and bury my father." And Jesus said to him, "Leave the dead to bury their own dead. But as for you, go and proclaim the kingdom of God."

We must work the works of him who sent me while it is day; night is coming, when no one can work.

Preach the word; be ready in season and out of season; reprove, rebuke, and exhort, with complete patience and teaching.

Therefore, as the Holy Spirit says, "Today, if you hear his voice, do not harden your heart."

Pray you therefore the Lord of the harvest, that He will send forth laborers into his harvest.

Jesus said to them, My meat is to do the will of Him that sent me, and to finish His work.

I am debtor both to the Greeks and to the Barbarians; both to the wise, and to the unwise. So, as much as in me is, I am ready to preach the gospel to you that are at Rome also. For I am not ashamed of the gospel of Christ; for it is the power of God unto salvation to every one that believeth; to the Jew first, and also to the

Greek. For therein is the righteousness of God revealed from faith to faith for as it is written, "The just shall live by faith".

Santify them in the truth. Your word is truth.

These are the things that you shall do: Speak the truth to one another; render in your gates judgments that are true and make for peace.

Then Pilate said to him, "So you are a king?" Jesus answered, "You say that I am a king. For this purpose I was born and for this purpose I have come into the world—to bear witness to the truth. Everyone who is of the truth listens to my voice."

And you will know the truth, and the truth will set you free."

When the Spirit of truth comes, He will guide you into all the truth, for he will not speak on His own authority, but whatever He hears He will speak, and He will declare to you the things that are to come.

Have I then become your enemy by telling you the truth?

And for their sake I consecrate myself, that they also may be sanctified in truth.

Even the Spirit of truth, whom the world cannot receive, because it neither sees him nor knows him. You know him, for he dwells with you and will be in you.

And the Word became flesh and dwelt among us, and we have seen his glory, glory as of the only Son from the Father, full of grace and truth.

I sincerely pray that the simplicity of these writings will strike a chord within each reader's heart and will provoke them all unto their divine calling and unto the righteousness of God. What a privilege it is to shed forth the simplicity of God's word with others. I pray that these writings will fall as holy seed upon the fertile grounds of the readers' hearts and will bring forth much fruit in their lives as well as in the kingdom of God.

Thank you and blessings upon you, your life and your ministries eternally.

Call to Duty Verses "Call of Duty

What does it mean to be called to duty for Christ? And is there a difference between our call **to** duty and our call **of** duty? Sure there is; and in simple terms here are some of the major difference between the two.

First and foremost, the call **to** duty is the general call that everyone hears from God but not all answer it. Many ignore it for whatever reason. However, we have been warned that the day we hear His voice, we are not to harden our hearts. We are also taught that we must choose ye this day whom you will serve. Therefore, the call **to** duty is merely God's invitation to each person to receive his forgiveness, regeneration, recreation, salvation and deliverance as well as His adoption of them into His divine family as His own. However, none of this happens until we "accept the invitation" and then take our oath of enlistment (Romans 10:9). After our oath of enlistment, our heavenly drill sergeant, the Holy Spirit, teaches us the laws, behaviors, doctrines and ways of this spiritual army we have now joined. In the meantime, your spiritual supply officer prepares and issues your service uniform, the full armor of God (Eph. 6:10-17).

Now that you have joined the army of God, been through spiritual basic training and received your initial supplies and uniform issue, you are now ready to be placed in a position of responsibility in the Kingdom. Unlike the armed forces of man, God has already predetermined your duty position (Jer 1:4-5) and has tailor-made you just for that position. He has literally designed you in a fail-proof mode which is purposed to assure you of success. And so He has taught us that in all of these things you are more than a conqueror. The reason for God's assurance in this matter can be found in Psalms 139:13-17. Here we see that God has painstakingly assembled us, not from the inside out, but from the spirit outward to the flesh and has completely equipped and prepared us our chosen destination.

Once we have answered our call to duty, been trained, supplied and released, we then step into the office to which we have been called. (Thus **I ordained you** a PROPHET unto the nations.) Now comes the call **of** duty. Each duty will have its callings, requirements, sacrifices and challenges for each individual. In order to fully carry out the requirements of your duty assignment, know that that assignment will, of necessity, place many requirements, demands, sacrifices, restrictions—in a word callings—upon your life. That is the call **OF** your duty. Your duty is a demanding one. It calls you into holiness. It calls you into sanctification. It calls you into righteousness. It calls you into forgiveness. It calls you into love. It calls you into study, fasting, prayer, communion and so forth. That is why we have to render our bodies a living sacrifice unto God for do so is our reasonable service. We can never answer the call **OF** duty if we do not first answer the call **TO** duty. And we will never answer the call **TO** duty if we do not take the time to posture ourselves to hear the soft and tiny voice of the Caller. While God is sovereign and in total control of His creation, we are yet free will agents to answer or ignore the call.

According to Romans 1:6 we are the called among all of the nations of the world. However, it should be no surprise that many are called, but few are chosen because God will only CHOSE to use those who have joined His army, been subjected to His training and preparation regiment, been issued a battle wardrobe by His warring angels, and have been SENT (chosen) by Him. Is there any question why the harvest is plenteous? Simple. Because the laborers (those who will answer God's call) are few.

As Paul wrote, "I marvel that yea re so soon removed from Him that called you in to the grace of Christ . . ." especially when you stop to consider **<u>Faithful is He that calleth you</u>**."

Blessings.

Printed in the United States
by Baker & Taylor Publisher Services